THE SAGES SPEAK

Rabbinic Wisdom and Jewish Values

WILLIAM B. SILVERMAN

Jason Aronson Inc.
Northvale, New Jersey
London

First Jason Aronson Inc. softcover edition—1995

Copyright © 1995, 1989 by William B. Silverman

10 9 8 7 6 5 4 3 2 1

Library of Congress Cataloging-in-Publication Data

Silverman, William B.
    The sages speak : rabbinic wisdom and Jewish values / William B. Silverman.
      p. cm.
    Previously published: New York : Union of American Hebrew
Congregations, c1971.
    Includes index.
    ISBN 0-87668-829-6 (hardcover)
    ISBN 1-56821-410-3 (softcover)
    1. Aggada. 2. Parables, Jewish. 3. Parables, Hasidic.
4. Hasidim—Legends. I. Title.
BM516.5.S55 1989
296.1'9—dc20   89-15142
                                                     CIP

Manufactured in the United States of America. Jason Aronson Inc. offers books and cassettes. For information and catalog write to Jason Aronson Inc., 230 Livingston Street, Northvale, New Jersey 07647.

In memory of my parents,
Simon and Rae Silverman

CONTENTS

PREFACE

The material used in this book is derived primarily from three sources: (1) the Midrash, (2) Talmudic literature, and (3) the teachings and stories of the Hasidic rabbis. There follows a brief explanation of each.

1. The Midrash

Midrash is derived from the Hebrew root *dorash* — to search out and investigate. It is an effort on the part of the rabbis to examine and interpret the text of the Bible and thus to penetrate more deeply into the understanding of God's will. The Midrash offers homilies, stories, and interpretations of Jewish law and ethics. Homilies based on Jewish law are known as Midrash

Halachah. Homilies based on ethical and narrative teachings are known as Midrash Haggada.

Throughout the centuries the Jewish preacher has made use of the Midrashic material in the exposition and development of his own religious message. The best-known and most important of the Midrashim (plural of Midrash) were compiled during a period of approximately one thousand years and are called the Midrash Rabboth, or the Great Midrash. These date up to approximately the year 200 c.e. and offer interpretations of the entire Pentateuch and the Five Scrolls.[1]

2. Talmudic Literature

The Talmud is the record of the discussion and the religious decisions of the rabbis extending over a period of a thousand years. It contains the prayers, customs, traditions, folklore, laws, legends, history, and ideals of the Jewish people. For thousands of years those of the Jewish faith have studied the Talmud and guided their lives by its teaching in the effort to interpret and obey the will of God.

The Talmud consists of two distinct parts: the *Mishnah,* and its commentary, the *Gemara.* The Mishnah was compiled and edited by Judah Ha-Nasi (Rabbi Judah the Prince) about the year 200 of the Common Era.

There are two Talmuds: the Babylonian and the Palestinian, both offering comprehensive interpretations of Jewish law and life. The Babylonian Talmud, which was compiled about the year 500 of the Common Era, became accepted as the authoritative source for Jewish living. A work of great erudition, it contains about 2,500,000 words. The Talmud is made up of Halachah, which deals with the law, and Haggada,

---

[1]Song of Songs, Ruth, Lamentations, Ecclesiastes, Esther.

which is concerned with moral narratives and ethical stories. This volume is limited to the stories and legends derived from the Babylonian Talmud.

3. The Teachings and Stories of the Hasidic Rabbis

The religious movement known as Hasidism was founded in the eighteenth century in eastern Europe by one who was known as Israel Baal Shem Tov, the "Master of the Good Name." The Besht, as he was known, was a pious and dedicated rabbi who emphasized not the letter of the law, but the spirit of reverence that enables man to draw near unto the Divine Presence. He and his disciples, the Hasidim, taught that the love of God is expressed not only through prayer, but through song and dance, by giving to charity, by kindness, compassion, and joyous service to one's fellow man. To the Hasidic rabbis, the love of God is the greatest joy, and obedience to His commandments, the greatest happiness.

The Hasidim heard the music of Judaism singing through their lives with the Divine melody of holiness. They taught that it is only when the love of God fills the heart and soul of man that he can lift himself to a sacred communion with the Most High. To those chained to the letter of the law, the Hasidic movement offered a new and rapturous opportunity to search for God and find God in a religion of joyous worship and exalted living.

Grateful acknowledgment is here made to the following:

My teacher, Dr. Israel Bettan, of blessed memory, professor of Homiletics and Midrash of the Hebrew Union College, Jewish School of Religion, in Cincinnati,

Ohio, who encouraged the author in the preparation of
this volume.

Schocken Books, Inc., for permission to use stories
from *Tales of the Hasidim,* by Martin Buber.

The Soncino Midrash and Talmud, for the excellent
translation of traditional stories, illustrations, and homilies.

The Jewish Publication Society of America, for the
story from *Kiddush Ha-Shem,* by Sholem Asch.

Chapter I

GOD

Any inquiry into the religious literature of Judaism must begin with God. The stories, legends, homilies, and midrashim of the rabbis were offered to assist man in his eternal quest for knowledge of the living God. At no time were the rabbis concerned with the story as a story. They were not hucksters of homilies, intent upon the exchange of intriguing narratives. The interpreters of Jewish law and lore were not storytellers, but teachers and preachers of the word of God.

※ A learned man approached Rabbi Baruch and said to him: "Now let us hear teachings from you, Rabbi. You speak so well!" "Rather than speak so well," said the Hasidic rabbi, "I should be stricken dumb."

※ Rabbi Michal once gave a sermon in which he said: "My words shall be heeded." And then he added in

1

haste: "I do not say: 'You shall heed my words.' I say: 'My words shall be heeded.' I address myself too! I too must heed my words."

🐟 A rabbi whose grandfather had been a disciple of the Baal Shem said: "A story must be told in such a way that it constitutes help in itself. My grandfather was lame. Once he was asked to tell a story about his teacher. He related how the holy Rabbi Israel hopped and danced while he prayed. My grandfather was so compelled by his story that he himself began to hop and dance to illustrate the actions of the Baal Shem. From that hour on he was cured of his lameness. That's the way to tell a story."

The Hasidim were concerned with moral lameness and through their stories they attempted to show their disciples how to walk and run swiftly in the ways of God.

🐟 The rabbi of Rizhyn said: "As when someone prepares to split a tree with an ax, and takes a great swing at it but misses, and the ax goes into the earth, so it is when the zaddik [righteous teacher] talks to people in order to rouse their hearts to the service of God, but they do not heed him, and admire only the cleverness and artfulness of his sermon."

The sermon was not to enable the preacher to demonstrate his oratorical skill. The story was not intended to embellish or enhance the effectiveness of the sermon. The story was the sermon. The homily, midrash, and interpretation were miniature sermons to advance man's search for the understanding of God's commandments.
But is it possible for man to attain an absolute knowledge of

*God and behold the radiance of the Divine splendor? This is
the question that is asked repeatedly. The rabbinic homilies
suggest that we approach God's omnipresence with humility.*

THE OMNIPRESENCE OF GOD

❧ "You teach," said the Emperor Trajan to Rabbi
Joshua, "that your God is everywhere, and boast that
He resides among your nation. I should like to see
Him." "God's presence is indeed everywhere," replied
Joshua, "but He cannot be seen; no mortal eye can
behold His glory." The emperor insisted. "Well," said
Joshua, "first we must attempt to look at one of His
servants." The emperor consented. The rabbi took him
in the open air at noonday, and bid him look at the sun
in its meridian splendor. "I cannot," said Trajan; "the
light dazzles me." "Thou art unable," said Joshua, "to
endure the light of one of His servants, and canst thou
expect to behold the resplendent glory of the Creator?
Would not such a sight annihilate thee?"

❧ The Emperor said to Rabbi Gamaliel: "You say that
wheresoever ten men are assembled [for prayer] God
comes to them. How many gods are there, then?"
Gamaliel called his servant and struck him lightly on
the neck. The Emperor asked: "Why did you strike
him?" "Because he let the sun shine into the house,"
answered Gamaliel. "But the sun is everywhere," said
the Emperor. And Rabbi Gamaliel replied: "The sun is
but one among the thousands and thousands of myr-
iads which are before the Holy One, blessed be He: yet
the sun is everywhere in the world. Much more so,
then, is the Holy One Himself."

A little boy was playing hide-and-seek with his friends. For some unknown reason they stopped playing while he was hiding. He began to cry. His old grandfather came out of the house to see what was troubling him and to comfort him. The grandfather said: "Do not weep, my child, because the boys did not come to find you. Perhaps you can learn from this disappointment. All of life is like a game between God and man, only it is God who is weeping, for man is not playing the game fairly. God is waiting to be found, and men have gone off in the search of other things."

God is waiting to be found—but where shall man find Him?

"Where is the dwelling of God?" the rabbi of Kotsk asked a number of learned men. They laughed at him. "What a thing to ask! Is not the whole world full of His glory?" The pious rabbi thought for a moment, and then he answered his own question: "Where is God? God dwells wherever man lets Him in."

If God dwells wherever man lets Him in, then man must sensitize his soul to behold God in every aspect of life.

When Rabbi Yitzhak Meir was a little boy, his mother once took him to see the Preacher of Kosnitz. There someone said to him: "Yitzhak Meir, I'll give you a gulden if you can tell me where God lives!" He replied: "And I'll give you two gulden if you tell me where He doesn't!"

The quest for God must be characterized by humility. It is not by a gigantic leap of faith, but step by step and measure by measure, that we draw near to the Divine Presence, only to avert our eyes from the piercing light, the resplendent glory of a mystery too awesome and too wonderful for us to behold or understand completely. Moses learned this when he turned his eyes from the burning bush. He was reminded of this again when he said: "Show me, I pray Thee, Thy glory." God said: "I will make all My goodness pass before thee." When Moses persisted in his yearning to behold God, he was humbled by the Voice that declared: "Thou canst not see My face, for man shall not see Me and live" (Exodus 33:18–20).

While mortal man may never completely know the immortal God, he is privileged to witness God's goodness pass before him. Finite man can never completely comprehend the infinite God, but he must ever quest for the Divine afterglow of God's nearness. The impossibility of his attaining complete knowledge of God does not release man from the holy commitment of continuing his search for the Divine. Chained like Prometheus to his destiny, man is not free to desist from the eternal quest. Man is compelled by his yearning for God even as Jeremiah, who reluctantly forces from his lips the admission:

> And if I say:
> "I will not make mention of Him,
> Nor speak any more in His Name,"
> Then there is in my heart as it were a
> burning fire
> Shut up in my bones,
> And I weary myself to hold it in,
> But cannot.
>
> —Jeremiah 20:9

Moses, the lawgiver, and Jeremiah, the prophet, both failed to behold the full radiance of God's being, and yet they knew that God was near. The psalmist never could attain to the complete knowledge of God, and yet he recognized that he could never escape from the Divine Presence, as he asked:

Whither shall I go from thy spirit?
Or whither shall I flee from Thy
presence?
If I ascend up into heaven, Thou art
there;
If I make my bed in the netherworld,
behold, Thou art there.
If I take the wings of the morning,
And dwell in the uttermost parts of the
sea,
Even there would Thy hand lead me,
And Thy right hand would hold me.

—Psalm 139:7–10

The lawgiver, the prophet, and the psalmist were allowed but a glimpse of the Divine, and yet, keenly aware of the limitations imposed upon them by their mortality, they persisted in their search to behold God's glory as it passed before them in every manifestation of life.

THE REVELATION OF GOD

The revelation of God to man is continuous and progressive. It is not limited to one faith, one people, one time, or one place.

God had intended to reveal His Torah[1] to Adam, but because of the weakness of Adam, God determined to bequeath the moral legacy of His commandments to the sons of Adam. Since the Hebrew word "Adam" means "man," this is interpreted by the rabbis to mean

---

[1]The Torah literally means "teaching." It applies to the scroll containing the five books of Moses. It is also used in a broader sense—to apply to Holy Scriptures and all Jewish sacred literature.

that God's will is universally revealed to the sons of man—that is, all the descendants of Adam.

When God gave the Torah on Sinai, He spoke and the Voice reverberated through the world. Rabbi Yochanan said that God's voice split up into seventy voices in seventy languages so that all nations should understand. Thus each nation heard the Voice in its own vernacular.

God's Divine law was not given in any one king's land, nor in any one city or inhabited spot, but in the desert, a vast space that does not belong to any land or any people, but belongs to God. This is to teach that the revelation of God is the inheritance of all mankind.

The Torah was not given to Israel alone. It was offered to all nations and peoples of the world.

"When God revealed Himself on Sinai, there was not a nation at whose door He did not knock, but they would not undertake to keep it. As soon as He came to Israel, they exclaimed: 'All that the LORD hath spoken will we do, and obey' (Exodus 24:7)."

At Sinai God revealed Himself through the Decalogue by means of a voice. In the rabbinic tradition God is also revealed through the creative grandeur of nature. The Divine Presence is manifest by the earth wrapped in green garments of verdant finery, through the luminescent glory of the sun, and the stars parading through the heavens in a celestial pageantry of unequaled wonder. This is what the psalmist meant when he proclaimed:

> The heavens declare the glory of God,
> And the firmament showeth His
> handiwork.
> —Psalm 19:1

God is not only manifest in the wonders and spectaculars of nature, but His presence is revealed in the miracle of a leaf— in the Divine potential within the humblest thornbush. The Bible reminds us that Moses beheld God in the bush that burned with fire and was not consumed.

A heathen once asked Rabbi Joshua ben Karhah: "Why did God choose a thornbush from which to speak to Moses?" He replied: "To teach you that no place is devoid of God's presence, not even the humblest thornbush."

Rabbi Eliezer said: "Just as the thornbush is the lowliest of all trees in the world, so the people of Israel were lowly and humble in Egypt; therefore did God reveal Himself to them."

God's will is revealed through scripture, through nature, and through man himself. God reveals Himself—even as a teacher and a father.

"Come and see that the ways of God are not those of men. A mortal king cannot rule and at the same time be a scribe and a teacher of little children, but God can do all these things. Even though He is the Creator of the universe and rules the world, He descended to teach His children Torah. Hence does it say: 'Behold, God doeth loftily in His power; who is a teacher like unto Him?' (Job 36:22)."

Moses was still a novice in prophecy; therefore God said to Himself, "If I reveal Myself to him in loud tones, I shall alarm him, but if I reveal Myself with a subdued voice, he will hold prophecy in low esteem." Whereupon God addressed Moses in his father Amram's voice. Moses was overjoyed to hear his father speak, for it gave him the assurance that his father was still alive.

The voice called his name twice, and he answered, "Here am I! What is my father's wish?" God replied, saying, "I am not thy father. I but desired to refrain from terrifying thee, therefore I spoke with thy father's voice. I am the God of thy father, the God of Abraham, the God of Isaac, and the God of Jacob."

We speak of God as our Heavenly Father, and yet how frequently we regard Him as the stern and awesome deity to be feared! The Midrash emphasizes the loving-kindness and the tenderness of a God who speaks to Moses in the gentle and familiar voice of his father.

This may also be interpreted to mean that God speaks to us through our parents. Rabbinic literature is replete with statements teaching that parents are in copartnership with God and serve as God's messengers to us on earth.

We take pride in our independence, but religion suggests that we make a "declaration of dependence" upon our Heavenly Father. Frequently we forget that God sustains us even as we speculate on His existence.

※ A small child is seated upon his father's shoulders. The child beholds a friend of his father and calls out: "Have you seen my father?" The father then says: "You are riding upon my shoulders and yet you inquire of my whereabouts."

In a simple homily we are made aware that even as we inquire, "Where is God?" our Heavenly Father is carrying us, sustaining us, and providing our very existence.

Man must constantly attempt to develop an acuity of spiritual vision to behold God. H. G. Wells acknowledged his own lack of religious vision in an autobiographical note: "There was a time when my little soul shone and was uplifted at the starry enigma of the sky. That has gone absolutely. Now I can go out and look at the stars as I look at the pattern of wallpaper on a railway station waiting room."

By contrast, commenting on the twenty-second chapter of Genesis, the Midrash inquires into the deeper meaning of verses 4–5: "Abraham lifted up his eyes, and saw the place afar off. And Abraham said unto his young men: 'Abide ye here with the ass, and I and the lad [Isaac] will go yonder; and we will worship, and come back to you.' "

🦌 Abraham lifted up his eyes and beheld the mountain of God in the distance. He asked Isaac if he too saw the mountain. When Isaac responded, "Yes," Abraham asked his servants what they saw. They looked and beheld nothing. Abraham then declared: "Spiritual vision is the gift that God gives to man. If ye cannot see God's presence, then ye are like asses. Therefore, since ye are like asses, abide ye here with the ass, and I and the lad will go yonder; and we will worship and come back to you."

It is the spiritual vision that enables man to lift his eyes on high to behold the Divine Presence—even afar off. This midrash may be applied to our hope and dream of God's kingdom on earth. Men and women of faith lift their eyes to that dream and are inspired by its Divine glory, even though it may be afar off. Others, like asses, cannot see and are content to remain on an animal level, while the dreamers advance up the mountaintop of divinity to behold the Divine Presence and worship in the beauty of holiness.

To the Hasidic rabbis God was not an absentee landlord of the universe. He was and is a personal God, accessible to all— a God who responds to the needs of His children.

🦌 Commenting on Exodus 15:2, "This is my God, and I will glorify Him; my father's God, and I will exalt

Him," a Hasidic rabbi said: "I can point my finger anywhere to the heaven or the earth and say, 'This is *my* God, and I will glorify Him.' It is not enough for man to say, 'God.' He must feel that he belongs to God, and that God belongs to him. That is what permits him to say, 'This is *my* God.' After he says, 'This is my God,' then he should exalt Him as his father's God."

⚜ The Hasidic rabbis ask: Why do the prayer book and the scripture refer to "the God of Abraham, the God of Isaac, and the God of Jacob"? Why not state: "the God of Abraham, Isaac, and Jacob"? Why is God repeated each time?

This is to teach us that the God of Abraham was not the same as the God of Isaac, and the God of Isaac was not the same as the God of Jacob. Each generation grows in its knowledge of God. Moreover, God reveals Himself anew to each generation.

This is what is meant by the progressive revelation of God. As science demonstrates the order and precision of the universe, and as man acquires more extensive knowledge of nature and the world in which he lives, the glory of God is enhanced, and the Divine Presence is made more reverently and wondrously manifest to each generation.

Every individual does not perceive God in the same way. Each individual differs in his capacity for God. How much of God can we take? How much of God's will are we capable of understanding?

⚜ "God comes to each one according to his strength. For know thou, if God had come upon Israel with the full might of His strength when He gave them the Torah, they would not have been able to withstand it, as it says: 'If we hear the voice of the LORD our God any more, then we shall die' (Deuteronomy 5:22). God, however, came upon them according to their individual strength."

If God comes to each one according to his strength, then man must ever seek ways to enlarge his capacity for God. The rabbis taught that we enlarge our capacity for God by means of reverence, love, the imitation of the Divine attributes, and by consecrated service to our fellowman. Just as a person enlarges his capacity for athletics by practice, so we must exercise our spiritual potential by practicing the ethical requirements of our religious faith. Through love, service, worship, and moral action, we enlarge our capacity to receive more of the inspiration of God.

REVERENCE FOR GOD

Man also enlarges his capacity for God by means of his love for God. It is through love, and not fear, that man shall know the Lord.

When Rabbi Yochanan, the son of Zakkai, was dying, his disciples visited him and entreated him to bestow his last blessing upon them. "Oh, may ye," said Rabbi Yochanan, "fear God as much as one fears a mortal king made of flesh and blood."

"Rabbi," said his disciples, "is this all, and no more?" "Oh," replied the dying sage, "would it were even so! Consider, my children, when a person commits a fault, does he not endeavor to hide it from his fellow creature, and say, 'If only no man seeth me. . . .' Would anyone be guilty of a crime were he certain it would be known? And what can be hidden from the all-seeing eye of God!"

There is truth to Rabbi Yochanan's observation, that man is more concerned with the fear of man than he is with the fear of God. When we are tempted to commit a wrong, we look about us to be certain that no one sees us. How do we reconcile this with the omnipresence and omniscience of God? Does not God witness everything we do? Does He not know our thoughts, both the hidden and the revealed?

While Rabbi Yochanan seems to teach the fear of God, the correct translation of the Hebrew word Yiroh *is "reverence" rather than "fear." In the English translation, through usage, we render the text, "Oh, may you fear God as much as one fears a mortal king." In keeping with the Hebraic tradition, however, it should be translated — "Revere God as much as one reveres a mortal king."* Yiroh *has the connotation of awe and reverence, rather than fear of God.*

The emphasis in the Jewish tradition is upon the love of God rather than the fear of God. God is the Heavenly Father. He is the One who entered into a covenant of love with Israel, saying:

> I will betroth thee unto Me for ever;
> Yea, I will betroth thee unto Me in
> righteousness, and in justice,
> And in loving-kindness, and in
> compassion,
> And I will betroth thee unto Me in
> faithfulness;
> And thou shalt know the LORD.
>
> —Hosea 2:21–22

It is through love — the love of husband and wife, the love of parents for children and of children for parents — it is by means of love for our Heavenly Father that we acquire a greater knowledge of God, and betroth ourselves to the Most High.

THE LOVE OF GOD

Judaism places more stress upon man's love for God than it does upon God's love for man. It is assumed that a Heavenly Father loves His children. Rabbi Shelomo, a Hasidic teacher, said: "If only I could love the greatest saint as much as God loves the greatest ne'er-do-well!" Jewish prayers, songs, and poetry attest to God's love for man. This is as unquestioned as a father's love for his children.

Since the moral emphasis of Judaism is upon man's love for God, the means of giving expression to that love is by obedience to the Divine commandments and by service to God's children.

Deuteronomy 6:5 declares: "Thou shalt love the LORD thy God with all thy heart, and with all thy soul, and with all thy might."

Rabbi Akiba defined the term "with all thy soul" to mean "even if He takes away your life." He attested it with his own martyrdom. When Rabbi Akiba was taken out for execution, it was the hour for the recitation of the Shema, and the sage proceeded with his prayer. His disciples said to him, · "Our teacher, you recite the Shema at this time?" He said to them, "All my days I have been troubled by this verse, 'with all thy soul,' which I interpreted to mean, 'even if He takes away your life.' I asked myself, 'When shall I have the opportunity of fulfilling this commandment?' Now that I have the opportunity, shall I not fulfill it?"

The Shema is the first word of the Hebrew sentence: Shema Yisroel Adonoi Elohaynu Adonoi Echod. Translated it means: "HEAR, O ISRAEL: THE LORD OUR GOD, THE LORD IS ONE." This is the watchword, the motto, and the foundation of the Jewish faith. It is the first prayer that the

Jewish child learns to utter. It is the last prayer the dying Jew repeats before he yields his soul to God. Historically, the Shema was repeated in every crisis. It is the Jewish affirmation of faith in God.

The Shema *is to be found in Deuteronomy 6:4. The importance of this statement is indicated by the fact that it is in every Jewish prayer service and precedes the prayer commanding the love of God:*

And thou shalt love the Lord *thy God with all thy heart, and with all thy soul, and with all thy might. And these words, which I command thee this day, shall be upon thy heart; and thou shalt teach them diligently unto thy children, and thou shalt talk of them when thou sittest in thy house, and when thou walkest by the way, and when thou liest down, and when thou risest up (Deuteronomy 6:5–7).*

This command has ever been interpreted as an admonition to apply God's commandments to life. Religion is not limited to one place or one day a week. Man is to implement the Divine commandments when he sits in his house, through the sanctity of family love, in every walk of life, in his thoughts as he prepares for sleep, and in his plans as he rises up to begin a new day.

Any rabbi or teacher of Judaism yesterday or today, asked to state the foremost principle of Judaism, must respond with the Shema and the prayer called V'ohavto—"and thou shalt love."

It is significant to note that in the Gospel according to St. Mark, Jesus responds to a query as follows:

And one of the scribes came, and having heard them reasoning together, and perceiving that he had answered them well, asked him, Which is the first commandment of all? And Jesus answered him, The first of all the commandments is,

Hear, O Israel; the Lord our God is one Lord: And thou shalt love the Lord thy God with all thy heart, and with all thy soul, and with all thy mind, and with all thy strength: this is the first commandment (Mark 12:28–30).

The second commandment, according to Jesus, is "Thou shalt love thy neighbor as thyself." This statement from Leviticus 19:18 is consistent with the Jewish tradition that teaches: The first and most sacred commandment is to love God. The second is the love of man.

It is only when the love of God fills the heart of man that he is able to elevate himself to a Divine communion with the Most High. If one has the love of God, he needs nothing else.

✌ "Once the spirit of Israel Baal Shem Tov was so oppressed that it seemed to him he would have no part in the coming world. Then he said to himself: 'If I love God, what need have I of a coming world?' "

This is not to be interpreted to mean that the Baal Shem Tov did not believe in a future life, or that he regarded its forfeiture lightly. He believed, however, that the love of God has precedence over any other consideration. One must love God without thought of reward, either in this life or in the world to come.

✌ There is a Talmudic teaching that Deuteronomy 6:5, "And thou shalt love the Lord thy God with all thy heart, and with all thy soul, and with all thy might," really means: "The true love of God is to serve Him with all your heart, with all your soul, and with all your might."

✌ The rabbi of Rizhyn said: "In certain prayer books we do not read: 'Cause us, O *Lord* our God, to lie down,' but 'Cause us, our *Father*, to lie down.' For when man thinks of God as God, whose glory fills the world and there is no thing in which God is not, then he is ashamed to lie down on a bed in His sight. But if he thinks of God as his father, then he feels like a fond child whose father sees after him when he goes to bed, and tucks him in, and watches over his sleep. Therefore, we pray: 'Spread over us the covering of Thy peace.' "

※ In expressing his love of God, the rabbi of Berditchev used to sing a song, part of which is as follows:

> Where I wander—You!
> Where I ponder—You!
> Only You, You again, always You!
> You! You! You!
> When I am gladdened—You!
> When I am saddened—You!
> Only You, You again, always You!
> You! You! You!
> Sky is You! Earth is You!
> You above! You below!
> In every trend, at every end,
> Only You, You again, always You!
> You! You! You!

※ In Roptchitz, the town where Rabbi Naftali lived, it was the custom for the rich people whose houses stood isolated or at the far end of the town to hire men to watch over their property by night. Late one evening when Rabbi Naftali was skirting the woods which circled the city, he met such a watchman walking up and down. "For whom are you working?" he asked. The man told him and then inquired in his turn: "And for whom are you working, Rabbi?"

The words struck the zaddik like a shaft. "I am not working for anybody just yet," he barely managed to say. Then he walked up and down beside the man for a long time. "Will you be my servant?" the rabbi finally asked. "For what purpose?" the man inquired. "To remind me," said Rabbi Naftali, "to remind me that I am working for God."

How may man work for God and demonstrate his love?

❦ The subjects of a king came before him and said: "Oh our King, we would show our love for thee. What shall we say unto thee? What gifts may we give thee?"

The king answered: "My subjects, I am grateful for your goodness in coming before me to show your love. But what words shall you utter? I know the sentiments of your hearts. What gifts may you give me? Am I not the king, the ruler of the entire realm? If you would show your love for me, attend to my words. I have children, and I cherish them dearly. If you would show your love for me, then go forth and serve my children."

When we come before God, the King of all Kings, to express our love by words and gifts alone, will this be acceptable before Him? We may imagine that God responds by saying: "I am grateful for the expressions of your love, but do I not know the sentiments of your hearts, both the hidden and the revealed? What gifts may you give to Me? Am I not the Ruler of heaven and earth? If you would show your love for Me, the Father, then go forth and serve My children."

The inference of the Talmud is that man expresses his love of God by prayer, ritual, and charity. While this is always acceptable before the Most High, we truly show our love of God the Father by loving-kindness and service to His children.

🦌 "Now, how shall man love God?" "This is answered in the words of scripture, 'And these words . . . shall be upon thy heart.' For by them thou wilt recognize Him whose word called the world into existence, and follow His Divine attributes.

"God is righteous; be ye also righteous, O Israel. Righteousness means love of truth, hatred of lying and backbiting. The seal of the Holy One, blessed be He, is Truth, of which the actions of man should also bear the impress. Hence, let thy yea be yea, and thy nay, nay. He who is honest in money transactions, unto him this is reckoned as if he had fulfilled the whole of the Torah."

🦌 Disciples of the maggid (traveling preacher) of Zlotchov asked their teacher: "In the Talmud we read that our Father Abraham kept all the laws. How could this be, since they had not yet been given to him?"

"All that is needed," the maggid said, "is to love God. If you are about to do something and you think it might lessen your love, then you will know it is sin. If you are about to do something and think it will increase your love, you will know that your will is in keeping with the will of God. That is what Abraham did."

Startling, and perhaps shocking to some, may be the declaration attributed to God in the Midrash: "Would that they had forsaken Me, but kept My commandments." In referring to the children of Israel, God does not ask for praise. The Holy One does not even ask the children of Israel to believe in Him. To believe in God without obeying His commandments is regarded as a mockery of the Divine. God's concern is not that His children affirm their belief in Him, but rather that they imitate His moral attributes by keeping His commandments.

THE ATTRIBUTES OF GOD

Judaism regards God not only as the Creator and King of the universe, but as the essence of moral perfection. While many scholars regard monotheism as the greatest contribution of Judaism, they err in their judgment. The greatest contribution of Judaism is not the belief in one God—monotheism— but rather the belief in ethical monotheism—*one moral God who demands morality from those who worship Him. The scriptural keynote of this Divine imitation is sounded in Leviticus 19:2: "Ye shall be holy; for I the* LORD *your God am holy."*

The rabbis amplified this by the following comment: "Even as He is merciful, so be thou merciful; even as He clothes the naked, buries the dead, and dispenses charity to all, do thou likewise."

"God's seal is truth," states a rabbinic maxim. It was pointed out that the consonants of the Hebrew word emet— *truth—are respectively the first, middle, and final letters of the alphabet, indicating that God is first, middle, and last in time, and that truth must be the beginning, the middle, and the end for man.*

Justice and mercy are also attributes of God. How does God exercise these Divine attributes?

⚜ A king had some empty goblets. He said: "If I put hot water in them, they will burst. If I put cold water in, they will crack." So the king mixed cold and hot water together and poured it in, and the goblets were uninjured.

Even so, God said, "If I create the world with the attribute of mercy alone, sin will multiply; if I create it with the attribute of justice alone, how can it endure? So I will create it with both, and thus it will endure."

The following stories reveal the rabbinic belief in the compassionate God:

✌ A respected woman once came to ask the advice of the rabbi of Apt. As soon as he set eyes on her, he shouted: "Adulteress! You sinned only a short time ago, and yet now you have the insolence to step into this pure house!" Then from the depths of her heart the woman replied: "The Lord of the world has patience with the wicked. He is in no hurry to make them pay their debts and He does not disclose their secret to any creature, lest they be ashamed to turn to Him. In His mercy He does not hide His face from them. But the rabbi of Apt sits there in his chair and cannot resist revealing at once what the Creator has kept secret." From that time on, the rabbi of Apt used to say: "No one ever got the better of me except once — and then it was a woman."

Man prays to God, but to whom does God pray? For what does God pray? This is the prayer the rabbis believed God addressed to Himself: "YEHI MOTZON MELFONAI"—"MAY IT BE ACCEPTABLE BEFORE ME, MAY IT BE MY WILL, THAT MY COMPASSION MAY OVERCOME MINE ANGER, AND THAT IT MAY PREVAIL OVER MY JUSTICE WHEN MY CHILDREN APPEAL TO ME THAT I MAY DEAL WITH THEM IN MERCY AND IN LOVE."

✌ A question was put to the rabbi of Radoshitz: "There is one sentence in the Talmud which we do not understand. We read: 'Whence do you deduce that God Himself prays? It says: "And I shall bring them to My holy mountain, and make them joyful in the house of prayer." It does not say, "their prayer," but "My prayer." And it follows from this that God Himself prays.'"

"How shall we interpret this?" asked a disciple. "Is the 'but' supposed to exclude the prayers of man?"

The rabbi answered: "Not at all. God takes pleasure in the prayer of righteous men. And more than that: It is He who wakens those prayers within them and gives them the strength to pray. And so man's prayer is God's prayer."

When the Egyptians drowned in the turbulent waters of the Red Sea, even as the angels rejoiced at the deliverance of the children of Israel, they turned to God asking, "Why do You weep, God? Rejoice, the enemies of Israel have perished in the Red Sea." The Merciful One chastised the angels gently, saying: "My children have perished. My children have perished. Shall I rejoice at the destruction of My children?"

Moreover, the Talmud teaches that God mourned for seven days over the fate of His universe before bringing the flood.

Once Israel Salanter, a pious rabbi, failed to appear in the synagogue for worship on the holy Eve of Atonement. The members of his congregation went out to search for him and found him in the barn of a neighbor. What happened to keep him from leading the congregation in prayer? On the way to the synagogue he found a neighbor's calf lost and tangled in the brush. Fearing that he might hurt the animal, he freed it tenderly and brought it back to its stall. He was asked: "How could you do that? Your first duty as a rabbi is prayer." The rabbi answered: "God is called *Rachamono*, Merciful One. An act of mercy is a prayer too."

Abraham Isaac Kook, former chief rabbi of Jerusalem, a sage, accorded loving-kindness to heretics, freethinkers, thieves, charlatans, and hypocrites, basing himself on the assumption that man is but little lower than angels, and that there is a spark of saintliness in every human being.

A disciple protested: "They don't deserve your time. They are taking advantage of your goodness." "My son," replied Rabbi Kook, "it is much better to be guilty of groundless love than groundless hate. We are commanded to imitate the attributes of God. If God has mercy upon all His creatures, should I close my heart and withhold my pity from any of God's children?"

☃ Rabbi Yose ben Durmaskit said: "Take as your guiding sign: Whenever you have compassion on your fellow, the Holy One, blessed be He, has compassion on you."

The Baal Shem said to one of his disciples: "God says, 'The lowest of the low is dearer to Me than your only son is to you.'"

☃ A calf was being taken to slaughter, when it broke away, hid its head under Rabbi Judah's cloak, and lowed in terror. "Go," said he. "For this wast thou created." Thereupon it was said (in heaven), "Since he has no pity, let us bring suffering upon him." And Rabbi Judah suffered for thirteen years. Then one day as the rabbi's maidservant was sweeping the house, she saw some newborn kittens lying there and attempted to sweep them away. "Let them be," the rabbi said. "It is written, 'And His tender mercies are over all His works.'" Thereupon it was said (in heaven): "Since he is compassionate, let us be compassionate toward him."

Through the Talmud, the Midrash, and Hasidic literature, Judaism reveals the belief in a personal God of justice and compassion. The rabbis found it difficult to reconcile a Heavenly Father, a God of love, with the concept of suffering and damnation in hell eternal. They could not think of a Merciful God as a theological executioner—a heavenly hatchet man irrevocably determined to cut us down, to punish, torture, and destroy us for our weakness and our sins. In their sermons and homilies they exhorted their people to direct their lives by the love of God. They taught their students to believe in the God who gives us the freedom of will to resist evil, to obey the moral law, to meet suffering with spiritual dignity, to sanctify life with holiness. Throughout rabbinic literature it is made clear that man shows his love of God by the imitation of the Divine attributes of justice and compassion. To speak of one's love for God and to disobey the moral mandate of the Holy One, blessed be He, constitutes blasphemy. Since God is our Heavenly Father, we most reverently demonstrate our love by consecrated service to His children.

Chapter II

MAN

A ccording to a Jewish legend, on March 2, 1580, just as the clock struck midnight, Judah Lowe of Prague proceeded with his plan to create a golem, a robot-man of clay.

Accompanied by two friends he went to the outskirts of the city, to the banks of the Moldau River, and found a bed of clay. Then he began to fashion the clay into the figure of a man. Working with desperate haste, chanting from the Sefer Yetzirah, the Book of Mystery, he formed the golem out of clay, and the robot lay before him with its face turned toward heaven.

Judah Lowe walked slowly around the clay body, from right to left. He looked, and behold! the body became red as fire. With growing terror in his heart, he saw the fire-redness fade from the body as water flowed through it. Hair grew on its head, and nails on its fingers and toes. But the golem was not alive!

The sages walked around the figure once again, and placed in its mouth a parchment with the name of God written on it. Bowing to the east and the west, the south and the north, all three recited together: "And He breathed into his nostrils the breath of life; and man became a living soul" (Genesis 2:7).

They looked again, and the golem opened its eyes. They said to it, "Stand up!" and it stood up.

Three men had assembled at midnight to create a robot-man, a golem. At daybreak four men walked homeward.

The place of the legendary creation of the golem was in Prague; the time, the sixteenth century. Almost four hundred years later, in the city of Cambridge, Massachusetts, scientists at Harvard University created a modern golem, a machine so closely resembling a human being that it was given a name—Mark II. This robot was called "the human brain." It could calculate figures into the billions in a fraction of a second. Mark could walk, talk, answer questions, and even work out the most complicated mathematical problems. Mark seemed to be a man in every respect but one—Mark lacked a soul. Mark could not distinguish between right and wrong. Mark was not created in the image of God, but in the image of a blueprint, in the likeness of a machine. The golem of Judah Lowe and Harvard's Mark II were both robots and not men.

Our own generation must answer the question, What is man? and determine whether man is to be assessed in terms of flesh, bone, sinew, the chemical elements on a valence chart, as a combination of atoms and molecules, as a robot that responds to stimuli, or as a sacred personality created in the image of God.

The ancient Hebrew psalmist had to answer this same question. He looked at the heavens and experienced an *overwhelming sense of awe before the wonders of God's creation, as he exclaimed:*

> When I behold Thy heavens, the work
>   of Thy fingers,
> The moon and the stars, which Thou
>   hast established;
> What is man, that Thou art mindful of
>   him?
> And the son of man, that Thou thinkest
>   of him?
> Yet Thou hast made him but little lower
>   than the angels,
> And hast crowned him with glory and
>   honour.

—Psalm 8:4–6

The psalmist knew that his answer to the question, What is man? would determine his attitude toward God, toward the world in which he lived, and even toward himself. And his answer was that man is a child of God, endowed with divinity through an immortal soul—and thus is but little lower than the angels.

That is the answer of the psalmist, but what is our answer to the question, What is man? Jean Paul Sartre, the existentialist, declares that "man is the incommensurable idiot of the universe." Bertrand Russell contended that "man with his knowledge of good and evil is but a helpless atom." H. L. Mencken insisted that "man is a sick fly, taking a dizzy ride on a gigantic flywheel."

Is man a lump of clay, a golem, a robot, a thing, a mass occupying space, or a priceless and precious child of God? Rabbinic literature reveals the answer to the question, What is man? in the following stories and homilies.

THE CREATION OF MAN

✻ "The Lord took dust from the four corners of the earth in equal measure. Some of the dust was red, some black, some white, and some as yellow as sand. These He mixed with water from all the oceans and the seas, to indicate that all races of mankind should be included in the first man and none be counted as superior to the other."

Why was Adam, the first man, created a single individual?

To teach us that whoever destroys one human soul, the Torah regards him as if he had destroyed the entire world, and he who sustains one human soul, the Torah regards him as if he had saved the entire world.

Also for the sake of harmony, in order that no man may say to his fellow man, "I am descended from better stock than you are." All men are descended from one common ancestor. Also in order that the scoffers may not say, "Many first individuals were created by many gods."

Also in order to manifest the greatness of the Holy One, blessed be He. Human beings mint coins bearing the picture of one original (a king or prince), and all coins are identical. However, the King of Kings, the Holy One, blessed be He, patterned all human beings after the image of Adam, the first man, and yet no two humans beings are exactly alike.

Because of all these reasons, every individual is privileged to declare: "For my sake was the entire world created."

✻ The Hasidim asked Rabbi Pinhas: "Why is it written: 'in the day that God created a man on earth,' and not 'in the day that God created man on earth'?"

He explained: "You should serve your Maker as though there were only one man on earth, only yourself."

It was a favorite saying of the scholars in Yavneh:

> I am a creature of God,
> My neighbor is also a creature of God;
> My work is in the city,
> His work is in the field;
> I rise early to my work,
> He rises early to his.
> Just as he is not overbearing in his
>   calling,
> So am I not overbearing in my calling.
> Perhaps thou sayest:
> "I do great things and he does small
>   things!"
> We have learned:
> It matters not whether one does much
>   or little,
> If only he directs his heart to heaven.

The Talmud

THE SANCTITY OF MAN

Rabbi Joshua ben Levi took a trip to Rome. He was astounded to behold the magnificence of the buildings, the statues covered with tapestry to protect them from the heat of summer and the cold of winter. As he was admiring the beauty of Roman art, a beggar plucked at his sleeve and asked him for a crust of bread. The rabbi looked again at the statues, and turning to the man covered with rags, he cried out: "O Lord, here are statues of stone covered with expensive garments. Here is a man, created in Thine own image, covered with rags. A civilization that pays more attention to statues than to men shall surely perish."

Such a homily illustrates the obligation of man to cherish and serve his fellow man. The motivation for such service is not compassion alone, but rather the conviction of faith that every human being is created in the Divine image, and thus is sacred and infinitely precious to God. When one neglects the appeal of a human being, it is as if one neglects the appeal of God. When we hurt or destroy a human being, it is as if we have hurt or destroyed a part of the Divine.

The body, since it houses the immortal soul of man, must not be desecrated or defiled. It should be kept clean and pure.

🔏 Once Hillel, the gentle teacher, concluded his studies with his disciples and walked forth with them. They asked him, "Master, where are you going?" He answered, "To perform a religious duty." "What is the religious duty?" they asked. He said to them, "To bathe." Said they: "Is this a religious duty?" "Yes," he replied, "if the statues of kings and theaters and circuses are showered and washed by the man who was appointed to look after them—how much more should I bathe my body which is the temple of the soul, as it is written, 'In the image of God made He man.' "

🔏 Rabbi Akiba said: "Beloved is man, for he was created in the image of God; but it was by a special love that it was made known to him that he was created in the image of God."

It is this special love of God for man that enables man to know that he is created in the Divine image. How should such knowledge affect man? It must teach him that since all men are created in God's image, there is a Divine relationship that makes us brothers. No man may arrogate himself above another, because all share in God's love.

While it is true that all are created in the Divine image, man partakes even more of the holy presence of God as he observes the moral and ethical commandments of God.

The sages said in the name of God: "I call heaven and earth to witness that whether it be Gentile or Israelite, man or woman, slave or handmaid, according to the deeds which he does, will the Holy Spirit rest upon him." We are also reminded by the statement of Maimonides (twelfth century): "Keep in mind that God requires the heart, and that everything depends on the intention of the heart. Therefore our teachers said: 'The pious among all peoples have a portion in God's love and in the future world.' "

It is because man has been given the intuition to know that he is created in the Divine image that he must sensitize his vision to behold his fellow man as "little lower than the angels."

The rabbis taught that the true worth of man may never be discerned from external appearances.

Once Rabbi Baroka walked through the crowded marketplace of his town and met Elijah, the wandering spirit of prophecy in Jewish lore. "Who of all this multitude has the best claim to heaven?" asked the rabbi. Elijah pointed out a disreputable looking man, a prison guard. "That man!" exclaimed the rabbi. "Yes," said Elijah, "because he is considerate to his prisoners and refrains from cruelty. His hope is to convince the prisoners to give up their evil ways and obey God's commandments."

Surveying the people rushing through the marketplace, the rabbi asked: "Who else is worthy of eternal life?" Elijah then pointed to two motley-dressed clowns who were cavorting ludicrously before an amused audience. The rabbi was astonished. "Scorn them not," admonished the prophet. "When not performing for hire, they cheer the depressed and the sorrowful. Whenever they see a sufferer they join him and by merry talk they help him to forget his grief." Therefore, we are taught: The heart ennobles any calling. A jester may be first in the kingdom of heaven.

MAN'S RELATIONSHIP TO GOD

The Hasidic rabbi Shelomo asked: "What is the worst thing the evil urge can achieve?" He answered: "To make man forget that he is the son of a King."

Just as a royal family may have a seal or crest of sovereignty, so man, the child of the King of all Kings, looks within for the seal—the insignia of his royal lineage. That seal is the Divine soul which attests to his spiritual royalty.

Man's relationship to God—Creator, King of the Universe, and Heavenly Father—imposes ethical obligations upon him. A prince or princess adheres to noblesse oblige *because of the relationship to the king. Man, as a child of the King of all Kings, must likewise maintain the conduct befitting his exalted relationship to God.*

A rabbi once said: "It is not that I am not tempted to eat forbidden food or yield to improper sexual desire. I am tempted to eat forbidden food. I am tempted to yield to improper sexual desire—but I must control myself, for the Lord has forbidden me."

Rabbinic theology specifies two impulses that struggle for supremacy within man: the yetzer hora, *the evil impulse; and the* yetzer hatov, *the good impulse. Man has the freedom of will to conquer the evil inclination by virtue of his relationship to God.*

🦌 A young man once told the rabbi of Rizhyn that he needed God's help in breaking his evil impulse. The rabbi's eyes laughed as he looked at him: "You want to break impulses? You will break your back and your hip, yet you will not break an impulse. But if you pray and learn and work in all seriousness, the evil in your impulses will vanish of itself."

Once the Baal Shem saw an acrobat walking across a rope. The crowd watched the acrobat with amazement, intrigued by his perfect balance and agility. The Baal Shem sighed as he said: "This man had to practice for many hours to control his body. Would that man so practiced to control his soul."
Man must concentrate on the effort to control his impulses.

🦌 Rabbi Hayyim of Krosno was watching a ropedancer perform. He was so absorbed in the spectacle that they asked him what it was that riveted his attention on this performance. "This man," he said, "is risking his life, and I cannot say why. But I am quite sure that while he is walking the rope, he is not thinking of the fact that he is earning a hundred gulden by what he is doing, for if he did, he would fall."

THE STRUGGLE AGAINST GREED AND EVIL

Man must constantly struggle against avarice and cupidity.

⅍ When Moses was a child in the palace of Pharaoh, the astrologers told the ruler that Moses would someday plot to destroy him, and that even now, as a child, Moses was endowed with cunning. "Let it be put to a test," said Pharaoh, as he ordered his servants to place before the child hot coals and a golden crown. "If he selects the crown, then I shall know that his fate is to destroy me. If he selects the hot coals, then I shall know that he is an innocent child without guile."

When the hot coals and the crown were placed before Moses, the child started to reach out for the glittering crown. An angel pushed his hand away, and Moses seized the hot coals. As children do, he put the hot coals in his mouth, and the searing heat did injury to his tongue and mouth. Pharaoh was satisfied that Moses had no designs upon his throne, and the life of the child was spared. However, Moses' speech was permanently impaired. Thus it is with man who must frequently choose between the allure of wealth and the work of God.

⅍ Rabbi Moshe Leib taught: "How easy it is for a poor man to depend on God! What else has he to depend on? And how hard it is for a rich man to depend on God! All his possessions call out to him 'Depend on us!' "

A religious teacher today could never accept Thorstein Veblen's acrid utterance: "One of the essential marks of decency today is to be ashamed of being a man of the twentieth century." One may be ashamed of individuals, but never of man. Contempt for man is an insult to God, who created man in His image. Recognizing that human beings are subject to temptations and unworthy desires, the evil urge constantly beguiles man, but God has granted the freedom of will, abetted by the "good inclination," to enable him to rule over it.

﷼ Commenting on the biblical verse "If thou wilt receive My words," Rabbi Judah b. Shalom said: "God said to Israel: 'When are you called My children? When you receive My words.' This can be compared to a king to whom his son said: 'Set some mark upon me in the land [that people should know] that I am your son.' Whereupon the king replied: 'If you wish that all should know that you are my son, then put on my purple cloak and place my crown on your head, and all will know that you are my son.' So God said to Israel: 'If you wish to be distinguished as My children, then occupy yourselves with the study of the Torah and with the precepts, and all will see that you are My children. So, when are you My children? When you receive My words.' " The more we obey the commandments of God as revealed through the Torah, the more are we worthy of being children of God.

MAN'S ETERNAL HERITAGE

The word "Torah" has various meanings. It is usually translated "the Law" and refers to the sacred scroll which is placed in the Holy Ark. Literally it means "teaching" and refers to God's teaching—the revelation of the will of God through the Bible and Talmud.

The following story illustrates the teaching that the lessons of the Torah are meant for man, and not for heavenly beings:

﷼ Moses entered heaven, and the angels said to God: "What does he who is born of woman here?" God's answer was as follows: "He has come to receive the

Torah." They furthermore said: "O Lord, content Thyself with the angels; let us have the Torah. What wouldst Thou with man, who dwells in the dust?"

Moses thereupon answered the angels: "It is written in the Torah: 'I am the LORD thy God, who brought thee out of the land of Egypt, out of the house of bondage.' " Moses further said to the angels: "Were ye enslaved in Egypt and then delivered, that ye are in need of the Torah? It is written: 'Thou shalt have no other gods.' Are there idolaters among ye, that ye are in need of the Torah? It is written: 'Thou shalt not take the name of the LORD thy God in vain.' Are there business negotiators among ye, that ye are in need of the Torah to learn the proper form of prayer? It is written: 'Observe the Sabbath day, to keep it holy.' Is there any work among ye, that ye are in need of the Torah? It is written: 'Honor thy father and thy mother.' Have ye parents, that ye are in need of the Torah? It is written: 'Thou shalt not murder.' Are there murderers among ye, that ye are in need of the Torah? It is written: 'Thou shalt not commit adultery.' Are there women among ye, that ye are in need of the Torah? It is written: 'Thou shalt not steal.' Is there money in heaven, that ye are in need of the Torah? It is written: 'Thou shalt not bear false witness against thy neighbor.' Is there any false witness among ye, that ye are in need of the Torah? It is written: 'Covet not the house of thy neighbor.' Are there houses, fields, or vineyards among ye, that ye are in need of the Torah?"

The angels thereupon relinquished their opposition to the delivering of the Torah into the hands of Israel and acknowledged that God was right to reveal it to mankind, saying: "Eternal, our Lord, how excellent is Thy name in all the earth! Who hast set Thy glory upon the heavens."

It is because the Torah was given to man, and not to angels, that man is all the more obligated to learn the Divine commandments and to apply them to life. It is man who has been blessed with the Divine potential to harmonize the nations of the world into one co-ordinated unit, not angels. Any effort to improve the world must begin with the individual man.

The rabbis taught that human values must always take precedence over property values. Because the generation that built the Tower of Babel had no respect for human life, catastrophe was visited upon it.

🌿 The Tower of Babel reached so great a height that it took a year to mount to the top. A brick was more precious in the sight of the builders than a human being. If a man fell down and met his death, none took notice of it; but if a brick dropped, they wept, because it would take a year to replace it. So intent were they upon accomplishing their purpose that they would not permit a woman to interrupt herself in her work of brickmaking when the hour of travail came upon her. Molding bricks she gave birth to her child, and tying it round her body in a sheet, she went on molding bricks.

They never ceased in their work, and from their dizzy height they constantly shot arrows toward heaven. Arrogantly they cried: "We have slain all who are in heaven." Thereupon God turned to the seventy angels who encompass His throne, and He spake: "Let us go down, and there confound their language, that they may not understand one another's speech."

Thus it happened. Thenceforth none knew what the other spoke. One would ask for the mortar, and the other would hand him a brick; in a rage, the first man would throw the brick at his partner and kill him. Many perished in this manner, and the rest were punished according to the nature of their rebellious conduct.

The Midrash thus points up the tragedy that ensues when a generation manifests contempt for the sanctity of human life and arrogantly strives to ascend to heaven to wrest sovereignty from God. Modern man should be mindful of this, particularly in the age of the Sputnik, when man-made satellites ascend heavenward.

THE FALLIBILITY OF MAN

Once Moses complained to God about the children of Israel, contending that they were stiff-necked and contentious. Thereupon God chastised Moses gently, saying: "I have not created them angels, but flesh and blood, fallible human beings. Therefore, do not expect them to act as angels. Since they are mortal, it is natural that they should have the imperfections and the limitations of flesh and blood, mortal human beings."

Judaism teaches that God is the only all-perfect Being. Man, by his very nature, is imperfect. He has the potential to perfect himself but may never be perfect. It is because man is bound by the limitations of his mortality that he must ever be regarded with understanding and compassion.

🦌 "Everyone must have two pockets, so that he can reach into the one or the other according to his need. In his right pocket are the words, 'For my sake the world was created,' and in the other, 'I am earth and ashes.' "

Man, the child of heaven, is created in the image of God and endowed with divinity by virtue of his immortal soul. He is also limited by his mortality and must ever concede that he came from the dust and must ultimately return to the dust. His soul, which is eternal and indestructible, returns to God to inherit life eternal.

Man is given the insight to behold himself as he is. Therefore, he must constantly evaluate himself in religious perspective, remembering the statement of Oliver Cromwell, who said, "A portrait should include all the warts." Usually when man looks at himself, he wants to see only his finer qualities. As God looks beyond appearances to the character and the soul, so man must be constantly vigilant in his evaluation of the warts and defects of character, with the purpose of correcting them.

Rabbi Hanokh told of the man who was very stupid. When he got up in the morning it was so difficult for him to find his clothes that at night he almost refused to go to bed, thinking of the trouble he would have on waking. One evening he finally took paper and pencil and, as he undressed, noted down exactly where he had put each article. The next morning, very pleased with himself, he took the slip of paper and read the list: "cap"—there it was and he set it on his head; "trousers"—there they lay and he got into them. And so it went until he was fully dressed.

"That's all very well, but now where am I?" he asked in great distress. "Where in the world am I?" He looked and looked, but it was a vain search. "And that is how it is with us," said the rabbi. When man asks, "Where am I?" he should always know that he is in the presence of God. Whatever he does is viewed by God. Whatever he says is heard by God. Just as the man in the story looked for his clothes, so man is adjured to ever search within himself, to correct his faults, and to purify his soul.

The arrogance that makes a man think he is perfect

takes him far from God. "There is no room for God in a man who is too full of himself" is the teaching of the rabbis. It is by filling ourselves with God that we are able to lose an undue preoccupation with self. "It is true that man must have time for himself," taught Rabbi Moshe Leib. "A human being who has not a single hour for his own every day is no human being." However, to take all the hours of the day for oneself is to invite selfishness and impiety.

Let no man think that his position in life will remain constant. Let no man become arrogant and believe that, because he is presently close to God, he will always remain close to God. Let no man think that, because he has alienated himself from God, he may never return to God.

Rabbi Nehemiah taught in a midrash: "Not everyone who is near to God is of necessity permanently near, nor is everyone who is far, of necessity permanently far. There are some who are chosen and rejected and then brought near; and there are others who are chosen and cast off and not brought near."

Life frequently demands resignation to the inevitable. Sometimes it is necessary to accept the troubles and anguish of life without struggling too much against one's fate.

When the son of the rabbi of Lentshno was a boy, he once saw Rabbi Yitzhak of Vorki praying. In amazement the boy ran to his father and asked how it was possible for such a pious man to pray so quietly, giving no sign of ecstasy.

"A poor swimmer," answered his father, "has to thrash around in order to stay up in the water. The perfect swimmer rests on the tide and it carries him."

Man is finite and his life is as a fleeting shadow. It is because of the brevity of life that each man must seek to perfect himself. The Midrash reveals how Adam learned about death:

Adam and his mate were seated weeping and lamenting for Abel, and they knew not what to do with him, for they knew nothing of interment. And behold there came a raven whose mate was dead, and he scratched out the soil, and took his dead mate and buried her, before the eyes of the man and the woman. Then Adam said: "I will do what the raven did." And he hollowed out the earth and placed therein the body of Abel and buried him.

The brevity of life and the fallibility of man must hasten the effort to do that which is pleasing in the sight of God. Each individual must constantly offer God the best that he has. This does not mean the offering of animals, or even words alone. What, then, is the proper offering to God?

Concerning the words of scripture, "When any man of you bringeth an offering unto the LORD," the rabbi of Rizhyn said: "Only he who brings himself to the LORD as an offering may be called a man."

To this end, those who call themselves teachers and servants of God must direct their efforts. Whatever work man does, there is no work more holy than that of religious education.

Once the rabbi of Kotsk told a wonder-worker who was versed in the secret art of making a robot: "That is unimportant. What is important is to know the sacred art of making a pious disciple."

🦎 "What was the true nature of Adam's sin?" asked the rabbis. Rabbi Yitzhak said: "Adam's real sin was that he worried too much about the morrow. The serpent said to him: 'What can you do to serve God? You are not able to distinguish between good and evil and thus you are unable to make a choice. Eat of this fruit and you will be able to choose the good and receive a reward.' " This, said Rabbi Yitzhak, was Adam's sin. He worried that he would not be able to serve God, yet at that very hour he had the opportunity to serve God, namely: to obey God and to resist the serpent. Resisting evil is also serving God.

THE MORAL DUTIES OF MAN

In all circumstances—in joy and in sorrow, in prosperity and in adversity—man must express his gratitude to God.

🦎 After God had created mankind, He asked the angels what they thought of the world He had made. "Only one thing is lacking," they said. "It is the sound of praise to the Creator."

"God created music, the voice of birds, the whispering wind, the murmuring ocean, and planted melody in the hearts of men."

This truth is emphasized by the psalmist in three successive hymns of praise and thanksgiving:

> O give thanks unto the Lord, call upon
>   His name;
> Make known His doings among the
>   peoples.

—Psalm 105:1

Hallelujah. O give thanks unto the
    Lord; for He is good;
For His mercy endureth for ever.

—Psalm 106:1

O give thanks unto the Lord, for He is
    good,
For His mercy endureth for ever.

—Psalm 107:1

"Thus the person who stops to think will also stop to thank. If we depend on Him in all things, knowing His personal love and care, true praise will well up in us constantly in every circumstance. Then every day, because of Him, will be Thanksgiving Day."

Because man is a child of God, and the seal of God is truth, man must constantly seek the truth.

When God was about to create Adam, he had already created the attendant angels, rank by rank and group by group. And there were some who said, "Let man be created," and others said, "Let not man be created." As it is written: Grace and Truth met, and Justice and Peace embraced. Justice said to God, "Create man, for he will give charity." Peace said: "Do not create him, for he will do nothing but quarrel." Grace said: "Create him, for he will do deeds of kindness." Truth said: "Do not create him, for he will do nothing but lie."

What did God do? He took Truth and threw her to the earth. And his attendant angels asked: "Dost Thou despise Truth, which is Thy seal? Let her rise again from the earth!"—as it is written: And Truth rises from the earth.

God does not expect men to be angels. What does God expect?

⛎ The rabbi of Kotsk explained: "It is written: 'And ye shall be holy unto Me.' What does this mean? It means: 'Ye shall be holy unto Me, but as human beings ye shall be *humanly* holy unto Me.'"

⛎ When Adam beheld the sun descend on the first night, he was terrified, thinking that light had disappeared forever and the sun would be seen no more. God, in His mercy, gave Adam the intuition to take two flints: the one, darkness, and the other, the shadow of death. He rubbed the two together and thus kindled a fire. Thereupon Adam uttered the benediction, "Blessed art Thou, O Lord, Creator of light." This is the meaning of the following verses:

> And if I say: "Surely the darkness shall
>   envelop me,
> And the light about me shall be night;"
> Even the darkness is not too dark for
>   Thee,
> But the night shineth as the day;
> The darkness is even as the light.

> —Psalm 139:11–12

Beholding the light, Adam was assured that darkness need not prevail and that the dawn would dispel the darkness.

This midrash has meaning and religious relevance to our generation beset by the fear of nuclear destruction. How many are those who yield to despair? How frequently is it said that darkness has forever seized the world in its black embrace? Religious faith must assure us as a generation and as individuals that out of darkness and the very shadow of death Adam created light. This was a portent of the greater light that would emerge with the dawn. Man must not despair because of darkness. When we draw close to God, "the night shineth as the day; the darkness is even as the light."

It is interesting to note that, according to the Jewish calendar, the day begins at sundown and not at sunup. All festivals and holy days begin at night. The Sabbath begins at sundown. According to the Jewish tradition, this is of moral significance. It is not difficult to have confidence in the day and to believe in the existence of light and sunup. The Jewish day begins at night to symbolize the faith, even in darkness, that light will prevail and that a new morrow will dawn upon mankind.

It is incumbent upon man to drive out the darkness from the world. As a child of God, but little lower than the angels, he is morally committed to combat evil, dispel the darkness, and identify himself with light.

The pupils and disciples of a Hasidic rabbi approached their spiritual leader with a complaint about the prevalence of evil in the world. Intent upon driving out the forces of darkness, they requested the rabbi to counsel them. The rabbi suggested that they take brooms and attempt to sweep the darkness from a cellar. The bewildered disciples applied themselves to sweeping out the darkness, but to no avail. The rabbi then advised his followers to take sticks and to beat vigorously at the darkness to drive out the evil. When this likewise failed, he counseled them to go down again into the cellar and to protest against the darkness and to shout imprecations to drive out the evil. When this, too, failed, he said: "My children, let each of you meet the challenge of darkness by lighting a candle." The disciples descended to the cellar and kindled their lights. They looked, and behold! the darkness had been driven out.

There are times when we, too, feel overwhelmed by the malevolent forces of evil in the world. As we attempt to sweep out the darkness and beat at the evils that beset us, perhaps we sometimes forget that the most effective manner of combating darkness is through the principle of light. The admonition of the Hasidic rabbi, urgent in its appeal, may apply to those in our generation: "Let each of you meet the challenge of darkness by lighting a candle."

Beginning with the command of God in the first chapter of the Bible, the principle of "Let there be light" has been a challenging motivation of the Jewish faith. Light has ever been a dominant symbol. When the land of Egypt suffered the plague of darkness, "all the children of Israel had light in their dwellings." At a later period the priest kindled the sanctuary flame in obedience to the Divine ordinance to keep a perpetual light burning upon the altar. The psalmist declared, "The LORD is my light and my salvation." Groping for certainty, faith, and direction, he prayed, "O send out Thy light and Thy truth; let them lead me." The practical sage of Proverbs insisted that "the commandment is a lamp, and the teaching is light." The God-inspired prophet exhorted his people, saying, "O house of Jacob, come ye, and let us walk in the light of the LORD." He insisted that if man would obey the Torah and follow the commandments of God, "then shall thy light break forth as the morning, and thy healing shall spring forth speedily; and thy righteousness shall go before thee." In the beautiful ritual observed in temples and synagogues today, the Sabbath lights are kindled with the declaration of faith: Light is the symbol of the Divine law. Light is the symbol of

Israel's mission. "I, the LORD, have kept thee for a covenant of the people, for a light unto the nations."

As we behold the darkness in our world and in our lives, shall we cry out in protest and lament the evil? Shall we yield to the darkness? Shall we beat at it with futile desperation? Shall we shout and protest against it? Let each individual, in his own way, make his contribution of light, and the darkness will ultimately be driven from the world. A living faith must, in the words of Swinburne, inspire man "to grow straight in the strength of [his] spirit and live out [his] life as the light," not only because God has created and made him, but likewise because God has created him in the Divine image and made him but little lower than the angels.

Chapter III

PRAYER

A learned rabbi was once asked: "What do you do before you pray?" He answered: "I pray that when I pray I may pray with all my heart."

Prayer is the bridge that enables man to approach God. It is a Divine conversation with the Most High. Man speaks to God, and God answers if the prayer is uttered in sincerity and truth. The rabbis were mindful of the psalmist's assurance:

> The Lord is nigh unto all them that call
> upon Him;
> To all that call upon Him in truth.
>
> —Psalm 145:18

🌿 "The Holy One seems to be far away, but nothing is nearer than He. Let a man enter a synagogue and pray

49

in an undertone, and God will give ear unto his prayer. It is as if a man uttered his thoughts in the ear of his friend who heard him. Can you have a God nearer than this, who is as close to His creatures as the mouth is to the ear?"

Rabbinic literature distinguished between prayer as a magical formula to propitiate the deity, and prayer as the sincere outpouring of the human heart in quest of God.

The poet W. H. Auden attempted to show how immature some prayers are, by writing a typical prayer of a childish adult—a modern Aladdin who thinks that all he has to do is to rub the cover of a prayer book and all his requests will be granted:

"O God . . . leave Thy heavens and come down to our earth of highways and aeroplanes. Become our Uncle, look after baby, escort madam to the opera, amuse grandfather. And please, God, introduce Muriel to a handsome naval officer."

This may sound shocking, but the poet meant it to shock, to jolt us into the realization that all too frequently when we pray we think of God as a Divine Genie who brings us the material benefits we request liturgically.

The prophet Isaiah warned against those who hypocritically appeal to God with prayers that are accompanied by immoral and dishonest actions:

> And when ye spread forth your hands,
> I will hide Mine eyes from you
> Yea, when ye make many prayers,
> I will not hear;
> Your hands are full of blood.
> Wash you, make you clean,
> Put away the evil of your doings

From before Mine eyes,
Cease to do evil;
Learn to do well;
Seek justice, relieve the oppressed,
Judge the fatherless, plead for the
  widow.

                                        —Isaiah 1:15–17

THE SINCERITY OF PRAYER

🦌 Once the Baal Shem stopped on the threshold of a house of prayer and refused to go in. "I cannot go in," he said. "It is crowded with teachings and prayers from wall to wall and from floor to ceiling. How could there be room for me?" When he saw that those around him were staring at him, he said: "The words from the lips of those whose teaching and praying does not come from hearts lifted unto heaven cannot rise, but remain to fill the house from wall to wall and from floor to ceiling."

Frequently we are inclined to the belief that the more eloquent the prayer, the more acceptable it is to God. The Hasidim refuted this by the following stories:

🦌 The saintly Rabbi Israel ben Eliezer, founder of Hasidism, taught that every heart can find its way to its Creator, if it goes out to Him in truth. The rabbi tried to make his devotions a complete surrender, as if he were offering his heart in his hands. Once on the Day of Atonement, he poured out his soul in prayer. But somehow he felt that genuine prayer was absent. Neither he nor any member of his congregation was able to offer it. The time for breaking the fast had long since passed. Yet he and all the devout around him were still searching their souls for the prayer that would find its way to heaven.

And so it happened that an ignorant shepherd boy came down from the hills. Attracted by the chant from Rabbi Israel's synagogue, he entered it. There he saw a group of men and women engrossed in their devotions. The boy felt a sudden urge to join in the prayers. In his childish way he did the only thing he could do— put his fingers in his mouth and gave out a long, shrill whistle.

The congregation looked up, scandalized; and the boy realized what a shameful thing he had done. But Rabbi Israel turned with a happy smile on his face to the congregation: "Our devotions are over. At last we were fortunate enough to offer an unselfish, heartfelt prayer in our midst."

There once was an ignorant, impoverished peasant who entered the synagogue for worship. He listened to the scholars and sages intone their beautiful prayers to God. Since he, too, wished to express his love of God, he ascended the pulpit and stood before the Holy Ark. The scholars and sages were astonished to hear this rustic repeating the letters of the Hebrew alphabet over and over again.

They nudged each other, commenting on this poor man's ignorance. They laughed and ridiculed him because he didn't even know the simplest prayers of the Jewish service. Then as the peasant began to speak, their laughter died in their throats, and their mockery turned to shame as they heard him say: *"Lord of the universe, I am a simple man—an ignorant man. Oh how I wish that I had the words to fashion beautiful prayers to praise Thee! But, alas, I cannot find these words. So listen to me, O God, as I recite the letters of the alphabet. You know what I think and how I feel. Take these letters of the alphabet and You form the words that express the yearning, the love for Thee, that is in my heart."* And thus saying, he continued to repeat the letters of the alphabet over and over again.

🦌 Rabbi Levi Yitzhak once came to an inn where merchants stopped on the way to market their wares. The place was far from Berditchev and so no one knew the zaddik. In the early morning the guests, one after another, quickly repeated prayers. When they had all prayed, the rabbi called the young men to him. When they came near, he looked gravely into their faces and said: "Ma−ma−ma; va−va−va."

"What do you mean?" cried the young men, but the rabbi continued to repeat the same meaningless syllables. Thus they took him for a fool.

Then he said: "How is it you do not understand this language which you yourselves have just used in addressing God?"

For a moment the young men were taken aback. Then one of them said: "Have you never seen a child in the cradle, who does not yet know how to fashion words? Have you not heard him make babbling noises, such as 'ma−ma−ma; va−va−va'? All the sages and scholars in the world cannot understand him, but the instant his mother comes, she knows exactly what he means."

When the rabbi heard this answer, he began to dance for joy. And from that time on, whenever on the Days of Awe he spoke prayerfully to God in his own inimitable manner, he never failed to tell God the answer given by the young men.

꿈 There was a certain man who was a herdsman, and
he did not know how to pray. But it was his custom to
say every day: "Lord of the world! It is apparent and
known unto You that if You had cattle and gave them to
me to tend, though I take wages for tending from all
others, from You I would take nothing, because I love
You."

Once a learned man was going his way and came
upon the herdsman, who was praying thus. He said to
him: "Fool, do not pray thus." The scholar then taught
him the benedictions, the recitation of the Shema, and
the regular order of prayers.

After the learned man had gone away, the herdsman
forgot all that had been taught him and did not pray. In
fact, he was even afraid to say what he had been
accustomed to say, since the righteous man had told
him not to.

But the learned man had a dream by night, and in it
he heard a voice that said: "You have robbed Me of one
who belongs to the world to come."

At once the scholar went to the herdsman and said to
him: "What prayer are you making?"

The herdsman answered: "None, for I have forgotten
what you taught me, and you forbade me to say: 'If You
had cattle . . .' "

Then the learned man told him what he had
dreamed, and added: "Say what you used to say."

Here we find neither Torah nor good works, but the
herdsman had it in his heart to do good and to express
his love of God. "The Merciful One desires the heart";
therefore, let men think good thoughts, and let these
thoughts be turned to the Holy One, blessed be He, in
love.

The sages taught: "When a soul truly desires God, it
already possesses Him."

THE NEARNESS OF GOD

The rabbis used prayer to praise, to confess, and to petition. Their primary objective, however, was to be with God and to experience the power and joy of a holy relationship with the source of all life. No prayer went unanswered. Where a man lifted himself to communion with the Most High, that in itself was a sacred and sublime experience, attesting to the truth of the verse "The nearness of God is my good."

Those who lead the congregation in prayer must ever be mindful of the nearness of God. They must resist the temptation of giving a performance before an audience and remember to lead the congregation closer to God.

🦌 In the congregation of Rabbi Levi Yitzhak there was a prayer reader who had grown hoarse. The rabbi asked him: "How is it that you are hoarse?"

"Because I have prayed before the pulpit," answered the other.

"Quite right," said the rabbi. "If one prays before the pulpit, one grows hoarse, but if one prays sincerely before the living God, then one does not grow hoarse."

Those who pray must ever strive to shut out disconcerting thoughts that interfere with the sincerity and intensity of religious devotion. The following story illustrates how even the most pious must struggle to keep their thoughts directed to God.

🦌 The disciples of the Baal Shem heard that a certain man had a great reputation for learning. Some of them wanted to go to him and discover what he had to teach. The master gave them permission to go, but first they asked him: "And how shall we be able to tell whether he is a true zaddik?"

The Baal Shem replied: "Ask him to advise you what to do to prevent your thoughts from straying as you pray. If the man gives you specific advice, then you will know that he belongs to those who are not honest. For this is the problem of men in prayer to the very hour of their death: *to struggle time after time with the extraneous* — to shut out the profane — and time after time to uplift and fit it into the nature of the Divine Name."

The Hasidim believed that the immanent God not only responds to the prayer of the leader, but that the humblest person in the congregation may bring the Divine Father into the lives of His children.

Every year on the Day of Atonement a woman came to Berditchev to pray with the congregation of Rabbi Levi Yitzhak. Once she was delayed and when she reached the synagogue night had already fallen. Distressed and upset because she believed that the evening service must be over, she entered the synagogue to discover that the rabbi had not even begun. To the astonishment of his congregation he had waited for her. When she realized this she was filled with great joy and prayed: "Dear God, Lord of the world, what shall I wish You in return for the good You have shown to me? I wish You may have as much joy of Your children as You have just now granted me."

Then, even as she was speaking, an hour filled with the grace of God came upon the world.

THE WILL OF GOD

Rabbi Mikhal gave this command to his sons: "Pray for your enemies, that they may be holy and that all may be well with them. And should you think this is not serving God, rest assured that more than all prayers, this is indeed the service of God."

A beautiful medieval prayer of the rabbis declares: "Lord of the world, I hereby forgive all who made me angry and caused me harm, whether they hurt my body or my honor, or my property, whether purposely or unwittingly, whether in deed or in thought. May nobody be punished through or because of me."

According to the rabbis, it is proper to express the yearnings and ambitions of one's heart, but it is God's will that must be done. That is why the Talmudic prayer usually begins: "May it be Thy will . . ." Rabbi Eleazar used to pray: "May it be Thy will, O Lord our God, to cause love and brotherhood, peace and comradeship, to abide in our lot; to enlarge our border with disciples; to prosper our goal with happy ends and fulfillment of hope. Fortify our good impulses in this life, so that the reverence of Thy Name be ever the longing of our heart."

Rabbi Chiyya would pray: "May it be Thy will, O Lord our God and God of our fathers, that none hate or envy us, and that neither hatred nor envy of any man find place in our hearts. Keep far from us what Thou hatest; bring us near to what Thou lovest, and deal mercifully with us for Thy Name's sake."

Rabbi Meir was troubled by wicked men who tormented him in many ways. On one occasion the rabbi was so disturbed that he beseeched God to punish them. It was then that his wife, Beruriah, said: "My husband, it is not written in the Psalms, 'Let sinners cease out of the land,' but rather, 'Let sins cease out of the land.' Instead of praying for the destruction of the sinner, why not pray for the destruction of the conditions that cause sin?"

The rabbis taught that he who fails to include his fellowman in his prayers is a sinner. For example: "If it is in a man's power to beseech Divine mercy upon another individual, it is a sin not to do so, as Samuel said, 'Far be it from me that I should sin against the LORD *in ceasing to pray for you' (I Samuel 12:23)."*

"Sometimes a man's prayer is not heard because he remained impervious to the troubles and needs of others, and thus has transgressed God's command: 'Thou shalt love thy neighbor as thyself.' "

One of the most exalted prayers in Jewish literature is the prayer uttered by the Hasidic rabbi Levi Yitzhak of Berditchev. The love of God dominates his every thought. His intention is to make every action an act of service to the Most High. Even his suffering must be dedicated to a holy purpose. That is why he lifted his voice to God, saying:

🦁 "Lord of the world, I do not beg You to reveal to me the secret of Your ways—I could not bear it! But show me one thing; show it to me more clearly and more deeply; show me what this, which is happening at this very moment, means to me, what it demands of me, what You, Lord of the world, are telling me by way of it. It is not why I suffer that I wish to know, but only whether I suffer for Your sake."

Such a prayer needs no commentary. It bespeaks more eloquently than words the grandeur of the soul of man as it seeks to understand and serve the will of God.

SHOULD WE PRAY FOR MIRACLES?

🦁 A great drought afflicted the land of Israel. The heavens were as brass, the earth as iron. Water dried up at the fountains and cattle dropped in the stall. The king called his people together, so that the nation might beseech the Lord to send rain upon the earth. Then the king stood forth and made his prayer, but the sky was as brass and the earth as iron. And the lords and great men, the wise men and chief captains, made their prayer; yet still the sky was as brass and the earth as iron.

Then there stood forth an old man, poor and in mean clothing, and he made his prayer, and lo! the sky was black with clouds, and there was a sound of abundance of rain.

Then the king and his counselors and his captains, the priests and the wise men, gathered round that poor old man, saying, "And who are you whose prayer has prevailed with God, so that He sends rain upon the earth?" And he said, "I am a teacher of little children."

This story exalts the position of the teacher. The title of "rabbi" means "teacher." The Jewish people could bestow no greater title of honor than that of teacher. The implication of this Talmudic story is that if anyone has the power to intercede with God, it is a teacher of little children.

Such stories of appeals for miracles, however, are not typical of the rabbinic prayer. Man should have faith in God and not ask Him to deviate from adhering to the natural laws He has created.

The following story graphically illustrates the belief that man should not rely upon miracles to attest to the presence and the power of God. There are manifestations of God's miraculous power all around us. A miracle does not attest to truth, neither does a wondrous act indicate that God approves or condones.

🌿 During a discussion on a difficult point of law, Rabbi Eleazer brought up all possible objections, but the other

scholars would not agree with him. Finally he said: "If
the rule is as I teach it, let this carob tree give a sign." The
carob tree moved back two hundred cubits. But the sages
said: "A carob tree proves nothing." So he said: "If the
rule is as I teach it, let the water in this channel give a
sign." And the water in the channel flowed upward
instead of downward. But the sages said to him: "The
waters of the channel prove nothing." Then he said: "If
the law is as I teach it, let the walls of the school decide."
And the walls of the school leaned over as to fall. And
Rabbi Joshua cursed the walls, saying: "When the pupils
of the sages dispute a point of law, what business is that
of yours?" Therefore, out of respect for Rabbi Joshua the
walls did not tumble; but out of respect for Rabbi Eleazer
they did not stand up straight again, but leaned over.
Then a Divine voice was heard: "What is the matter with
you? Why do you importune Rabbi Eleazer? The rule has
always been what he teaches it to be." But Rabbi Joshua,
rising to his feet, exclaimed: "It is not in heaven!" (Deuteronomy 30:12).

What did he mean by these words? He meant that the
Torah is no longer in heaven; it was given to us from
Mount Sinai, once for all time, and we need no longer
pay heed to a Divine voice, for in the Torah, given at
Sinai, it is written: "The opinion of the majority shall
prevail."

The prophet Elijah appeared to Rabbi Nathan, who
asked him: "What was God doing at that moment
[when Rabbi Joshua denied the value of miracles]?"
And the prophet replied: "God was laughing and
saying: 'My children have conquered Me, My children
have conquered Me.' "

*There is no irreverence suggested by the statements of either
Rabbi Eleazer or Rabbi Joshua. The story is not to be taken*

literally. It is in consonance with the rabbinic method of teaching by means of a homily.

Rabbi Joshua points out that voices and visions, mysteries and apparent miracles that contravene the moral law of the Torah, may be ignored. God has revealed His Divine will through the Torah, and it is incumbent upon man to obey God's commandments. Those who invoke a miracle by means of incantations or prayers arrogate to themselves a supernatural power and interfere with the orderly process of God's natural laws.

Man should not pray to God to change things. Man's prayer to God should be a supplication for the Divine inspiration that will enable man to change things — to eradicate injustice and to create a world of justice, truth, and peace.

WORSHIP WITHOUT WORDS

In the Jewish tradition there are three methods of praying. The first is the articulation of our hopes and aspirations. This expression of prayer may be audible or silent. Not only may "the words of my mouth" but likewise may "the meditation of my heart" be acceptable unto God. We have already studied examples of such verbal prayer.

The second is study. The student who pores over the meaning of Bible or Talmud, seeking a greater understanding of God's will, fulfills a requirement of prayer even though he may not utter a single word.

Rabbi Levi said: "A harp was suspended above David's bed; and when the time of midnight arrived, a north wind blew upon it so that it produced melody of its own accord. [That is what is stated, 'When the instrument played,' that is, the harp played of its own accord.] When David heard its sound, he rose and engaged in the study of the Torah; and when the Israelites heard the sound of David engaged in the study of the Torah, they used to say, 'If David, king of Israel, is engaged in the study of the Torah, how much more should we be!' They forthwith rose and engaged in study of the Torah."

The third is the doing of good deeds. It is prayer in action. An act of loving-kindness is regarded as an equivalent of prayer. This is considered to be worship without words — and a manifestation of one's love of God.

The poet Whittier understood this third concept of prayer when he wrote:

> O brother man! fold to thy heart thy
>   brother;
> Where pity dwells, the peace of God is
>   there;
> To worship rightly is to love each other,
> Each smile a hymn, each kindly deed a
>   prayer.

A long time before Whittier, Judaism regarded ma-aseem toveem *(good deeds) as prayers without words. A man could speak with God, and the "still small voice" would answer through his deeds.*

The Hebrew word for worship is avodah. *This is derived from the root verb "to serve" or "to work." We must apply our religious faith and put our convictions to work. It is through service to man and God that we offer the most exalted of all prayers.*

The purpose of prayer is to bring us near to God. The nearness of God inspires us to deeds of loving-kindness and compassion. It is through prayer that we are challenged to imitate the Divine attributes by our ethical actions.

❀ When Moses said to the children of Israel: "After the LORD shall ye walk," they answered: "How is it possible for a mere mortal to walk in His ways?" Moses replied: "You misunderstand the true meaning of these words. 'To walk in His ways' means to emulate His Moral Being, for 'all the paths of the LORD are mercy and truth.' "

This applies to prayer. One should pray for the strength of will and the insight to emulate the moral attributes of God by following ways of justice, mercy, and love.

❀ A tale is told of one who sat in study before the zaddik Rabbi Mordecai of Nadvorna, of blessed memory (nineteenth century), and who, before Rosh Hashanah (the Jewish New Year), came to obtain permission to be dismissed. That zaddik said to him, "Why are you hurrying?"

Said he to him, "I am a reader of the service, and I must look into the festival prayer book and put my prayers in order."

The zaddik said to him, "The prayer book is the same as it was last year. But it would be better for you to look into your deeds and put yourself in order."

❀ A learned rabbi was studying when he heard an itinerant tailor pass under his window shouting: "Have you anything to mend? Have you anything to mend?" The rabbi examined his garments and said to the tailor: "My son, I'm sorry. I have nothing to mend." Then he clasped his hand to his mouth as he was struck by a thought: "I have nothing to mend? Here the high holy days are almost upon me, and I still have not mended myself." Thereupon he prayed devoutly but also sought to make repentance by deeds of kindness and mercy.

In the notes of Rabbi Moshe Teitelbaum made on the dreams he had in his youth, we find the following:

🦁 "I was looking out of the window on the eve of the New Year, and there were the people running to the house of prayer, and I saw that they were driven by the fear of the day of judgment. And I said to myself: 'God be thanked, I have been doing the right thing all through the year! I have studied right and prayed right, so I do not have to be afraid!' And then my dreams showed me all my good works. I looked and looked: They were torn, ragged, ruined! And at that instant I woke up. Overcome with fear I ran to the house of prayer along with the rest."

🦁 On the eve of a holy day all the Hasidim were gathered together in the house of prayer, waiting for the rabbi. But time passed and he did not come. Then one of the women of the congregation said to herself: "I guess it will be quite a while before they begin, and I was in such a hurry and my child is alone in the house. I'll just run home and look after him to make sure he hasn't awakened. I can be back in a few minutes."

She ran home and listened at the door. Everything was quiet. Softly she turned the knob and put her head into the room—and there stood the rabbi holding her child in his arms. He had heard the child crying on his way to the house of prayer, and had played with it and sung to it until it fell asleep.

THE DIVINE DIALOGUE

The Talmud designates prayer as "the Divine service of the heart." Rabbi Simeon insisted that "one should not regard prayer as a fixed, mechanical task, but as an appeal for mercy and grace." Other teachers insisted that one should pray only when one has a longing to do so in one's own heart and is attuned to it by reason of a devotional mood.

Prayer must ever be regarded as sacred because it is a "Divine dialogue." Man speaks to his Heavenly Father, and God answers with light, courage, and hope.

Illustrative of this is the incident related in Solomon Ibn Verga's book Shevet Yehudah:

"I heard from some of the elders who came out of Spain that one of the boats was infested with the plague, and the captain of the boat put the Jewish passengers ashore at some uninhabited place. And there most of them died of starvation, while some of them gathered up all their strength to set out on foot in search of some settlement.

"There was a certain Jew who struggled on afoot together with his wife and two children. The wife grew faint and died, because she was not accustomed to so much difficult walking. The husband carried his children along until both he and they fainted from hunger. When he regained consciousness, he found that his two children had died.

"In great grief he rose to his feet and said: 'O Lord of all the universe, You are doing a great deal that I might even desert my faith. But know You of a certainty that— even against the will of heaven—a Jew I am and a Jew I shall remain. And neither that which You have brought upon me nor that which You will yet bring upon me will be of any avail. It will not weaken my love of You or my faith.'

"Thereupon he gathered some earth and some grass, and covered the boys, and went forth in search of a settlement to begin a new life."

The Jew in this story was not being defiant. He felt free to express his indignation and sorrow—even to God. His prayer enabled him to go on with the assurance that God would yet lead him into a future of renewed life and hope.

✡ Rabbi Menahem Mendel of Vorki was asked what constitutes a true Jew. He said: "Three things are fitting for us: upright kneeling, silent screaming, motionless dance." What does this mean? It may be interpreted as follows: (1) *Upright kneeling.* Even when a Jew is standing upright, his heart must be prostrated in reverence before God. Everything in life must engender a feeling of God's presence. Even when he stands in the market place. Even when he walks by the way. (2) *Silent screaming.* In adversity, and in sorrow, when a scream of despair would issue forth from the throat, man must be silent and trust in the righteousness, the wisdom, and the justice of God. (3) *Motionless dance.* Even when a Jew remains motionless, his soul must dance in joy before the wonder and glory of God.

THE DEMOCRACY OF PRAYER

There is no power greater than God. There is no king more sovereign than the King of all Kings. Therefore, when a man goes before God in prayer, he must render God honor and not defer to the presence of scholars, noblemen, or kings.

✡ In his youth Rabbi Hanokh of Alexander was in the habit of praying with extreme gestures and loud cries, quite differently from Rabbi Bunam, who spoke with composure and calm, even when he conducted the services for the congregation. Once young Hanokh was praying when the rabbi entered the room, and the youth immediately lowered his voice and stopped gesturing. Hardly had he done this, when Hanokh reflected and said to himself: "Should I be concerned with the approval of the rabbi? I am standing and praying before God, not the rabbi." Thereupon he resumed his stormy manner of praying.

After the service Rabbi Bunam had him summoned. "Hanokh," he said, "today I was greatly pleased with your praying."

Rabbi Judah ben Sholom said in the name of Rabbi Eleazar: "If a poor man says anything, one pays little regard; but if a rich man speaks, immediately he is heard and listened to. Before God, however, all are equal—slaves, poor, and rich. How do we know this? Because of Moses, the greatest of the prophets. What is said of Moses is also said of a poor man. Of Moses it is written, 'a Prayer of Moses the man of God' (Psalm 90:1). And of a poor man it says, 'a Prayer of the afflicted, when he fainteth, and poureth out his complaint before the Lord' (Psalm 102:1). In both cases the word 'prayer' is used to speak before God. Hence, all are equal in prayer."

Rabbi Nahman of Bratzlav used to pray for all the peoples and nations of the world; then he would conclude by imploring: "May it be Thy will, O God, to extend peace, great and wondrous, in the universe. Let all the peoples of the earth recognize and know the innermost truth; that we are not come into this world for quarrel and division, nor for hate and jealousy, contrariness and bloodshed; but we are come into this world to recognize and know Thee. Be Thou blessed forever."

Chapter IV

HOLINESS

When man appears before the throne of judgment, the first question he is asked is not, "Have you believed in God?" or "Have you prayed?" or "Have you performed the ritual properly?" but "Have you been honorable and faithful in all your dealings with your fellow man?"

PERSONAL ATTRIBUTES OF HOLINESS

At the heart of rabbinic ethics is the concept of holiness. The goal of Jewish aspiration is not happiness, but holiness. It is through holiness that man achieves the maximum in a moral relationship with God and his fellow man.

Contrary to the prevailing supposition, holiness is not a vague, nebulous, pietistic, mystical state of being that enables

a man to withdraw from the world and limit himself to prayer
and ritual alone. "Ye shall be holy" is a commandment of God.
To obey this Divine admonition, man must perfect himself
ethically in his relationship with his fellow creatures.

The command "to be holy" has its source in the nineteenth
chapter of Leviticus, beginning with the second verse: "Ye
shall be holy; for I the LORD your God am holy."

It is significant to note that there follow the requisites of
holiness: respect for parents, the observance of the Sabbath,
consideration for the poor and the afflicted, honesty, justice,
equality, truth, sexual purity, assistance to those being
attacked or oppressed, and abstinence from vengeance. The list
of moral requisites for holiness culminates in the commandment "Thou shalt love thy neighbor as thyself." It is by the
observance of these moral precepts that man achieves holiness.
He deprives himself of this sacred opportunity when he
isolates himself from society and the problems of life.

The following story from Jewish tradition illustrates the
rabbinic attitude toward asceticism:

A student of Torah came to his teacher and announced that, in his opinion, he was qualified for
ordination as a rabbi. "What are your qualifications?"
asked the sage. The student replied: "I have disciplined
my body so that I can sleep on the ground, eat the grass
of the field, and allow myself to be whipped three times
a day."

"See yonder white ass," said the teacher, "and be
mindful that it sleeps on the ground, eats the grass of
the field, and is whipped no less than three times daily.
Up to the present, you may qualify to be an ass, but
certainly not a rabbi."

The flagellation of the body is not regarded as a mark of
virtue, nor is the mortification of the flesh considered to be a
requirement of holiness.

❧ The Torah teaches man to sanctify life with holiness through deeds befitting a child of God. It does not require asceticism or withdrawal from the world. According to Rabbi Pinchas of Korets, "Whoever says the words of the Torah are one thing and the words of the world another, may be regarded as a man who denies God."

❧ Rabbi Baruch of Mezebob, the grandson of the Baal Shem, records the answer given by his grandfather to the question which was put to him on fasting as a way of serving God.

"Fasting is not the only way," said the Baal Shem. "A man should take into his heart three things: the love of God, the love of Israel, and the love of the Torah. He does not need to engage in ascetic practices. It is sufficient for the average man to understand that in all things, physical and material, there is holiness."

To achieve holiness each individual must seek to perfect himself in the ways of God: How shall he begin?

❧ The Rabbi of Zans used to say about himself: "In my youth when I was filled with the love of God, I thought I could convert the whole world to God, but soon I discovered that it would be quite enough to convert the people who dwelled in my own town, and I tried for a long time but did not succeed. Then I realized that I was still too ambitious, and so I concentrated on the members of my family. But I could not convert them either. Finally, I realized that I must work on myself, so that I might give true service to God, but I did not accomplish even this."

❧ Commenting on the scriptural verse "I stood between the LORD and you" (Deuteronomy 5:5), Rabbi

Mikhal said: "The 'I' stands between God and us. When a man puts undue emphasis upon 'I,' he puts a wall between himself and God. However, he who offers his 'I'—there is nothing between him and his Creator. It is to him that the verse applies: 'I am my beloved's, and his desire is toward me.' When my 'I' has become my beloved's (God's), and my desire is God, then does He turn toward me in love."

❧ Before his death Rabbi Zusya wept as he said: "In the coming world God will not ask me: 'Why were you not as Moses?' because I am not Moses. God will not ask me: 'Why were you not as Isaiah?' because I am not Isaiah." "Why then do you weep?" queried his disciples. Rabbi Zusya sighed as he answered: "It is because God will ask me: 'Why were you not Zusya?' Have I lived up to the best that is in me? What shall I answer?"

Man, then, must begin his quest for holiness by improving himself morally and ethically. By his actions he acquires a good name.

"A good name is better than precious oil" (Ecclesiastes 7:1). Good oil flows downward, while a good name ascends. Good oil is transient, while a good name endures forever. Good oil is spent, while a good name is not spent. Good oil is bought with money, while a good name is free of cost. Good oil is applicable only to the living, while a good name is applicable to the living and the dead. Good oil can be acquired only by the rich, while a good name can be acquired by poor and rich. The scent of good oil is diffused from the bedchamber to the dining hall, while a good name is diffused from one end of the world to the other.

❧ Rabbi Simeon ben Shetah once bought an ass from an Ishmaelite. His disciples came and found a precious stone suspended from its neck. They said to him: "Master, 'The blessing of the LORD, it maketh rich' " (Proverbs 10:22). Rabbi Simeon ben Shetah replied: "I have purchased an ass, but I have not purchased a precious stone." He then went and returned it to the Ishmaelite, and the latter exclaimed of him, "Blessed be the Lord God of Simeon ben Shetah."

This midrash points up the obligation of living ethically to glorify God. Rabbi Simeon ben Shetah insisted that a man must be as scrupulously honest in dealing with a stranger or an enemy as one is in dealing with a friend. Significantly, the Ishmaelite did not praise the rabbi. Rather did he praise the God of the rabbi, knowing that it was the belief in a moral God that prompted Rabbi Simeon ben Shetah to return the precious stone.

The Greek may have been concerned with beauty and aesthetic form. The Jew, however, was concerned with goodness. Ethics had precedence over aesthetics. The verse "and God saw that it was good" is repeated in the story of creation, say the rabbis, in order to show the importance of goodness. God did not say that the world was beautiful—but God saw the light, the earth, the waters, and the work of His hands, and behold everything that He had made was "very good."

It is moral character, and not physical beauty, that leads to holiness. One does not judge inner worth by external appearances.

Rabbi Joshua, the son of Hananiah, was a man of ugly appearance. He was so dark that people often took him for a blacksmith, and so plain as almost to frighten children. Yet his great learning, wit, piety, and wisdom had procured him not only the love and respect of the people, but even the favor of the Emperor Trajan.

Since the rabbi was often at court, one of the princesses rallied him on his want of beauty. "How comes it," said she, "that such glorious wisdom is enclosed in so mean a vessel?" The rabbi, in no way dismayed, requested her to tell him in what sort of vessels her father kept his wine. "Why, in earthen vessels, to be sure," replied the princess. "Oh!" exclaimed the witty rabbi, "this is the way ordinary people do; an emperor's wine ought to be kept in the more precious vessels."

The princess, thinking him in earnest, ordered a quantity of wine to be emptied out of the earthen jars into gold and silver vessels; but to her great surprise, she found it, in a very short time, sour and unfit to drink.

"Very fine advice indeed, Joshua, hast thou given me!" said the princess the next time she saw him; "do you know the wine is sour and spoiled?" "Thou art then convinced," said the rabbi, "that wine keeps best in plain and mean vessels. It is even so with wisdom." "But," continued the princess, "I know many persons who are both wise and handsome." "True," replied the sage, "but they would, most probably, be still wiser[1] were they less handsome."

⚘ Rabbi Simeon, the son of Eleazar, returning from his master's residence to his native place, was highly elated with the great knowledge he had acquired. On his way he overtook a singularly dwarflike and ugly person, who was traveling to the same town. The stranger saluted him by saying, "Peace be upon thee, Rabbi."

Instead of returning the greeting, Simeon, proud of his learning, noticed only the traveler's deformity and,

---

[1]When the rabbis refer to "wisdom," it is to be interpreted as religious learning, and not academic or secular attainment.

by way of joke, said to him, "Are the inhabitants of thy town all as misshapen and ugly as thou art?" The stranger, astonished at Simeon's want of manners, and provoked by his insult, replied, "I do not know; but thou hadst better make these inquiries of the great Artist that made me."

The rabbi perceived his error and, alighting from the animal on which he rode, threw himself at the stranger's feet, asking for his pardon. "No," said the dwarf, "go first to the Craftsman that made me, and tell him, 'Great Craftsman, Oh! what an ugly vessel thou hast produced!'" Simeon continued his entreaties; the stranger persisted in his refusal.

In the meantime they arrived at the rabbi's native city. The inhabitants, being apprised of his arrival, came in crowds to meet him, exclaiming, "Peace be upon thee, Rabbi! Welcome, our Instructor!"

"Whom do ye call rabbi?" asked the stranger. The people pointed to Simeon. "And him ye honor with the name of rabbi!" continued the poor man. "Oh! may Israel not produce many like him!" He then related what had happened. "He has done wrong; he is aware of it," said the people. "Do forgive him; for he is a great man, well versed in the law."

The stranger then forgave Simeon and intimated that his long refusal had no other object than that of impressing the rabbi with the impropriety of judging from appearances. The learned Simeon thanked him; and during his lifetime he held out his own conduct as a warning to the people, saying: "A person ought ever to be as flexible as a reed, and not as stubborn as a cedar."

It is only when we bend as the reed that we are able to behold all men as the creation of the Divine.

THE REQUIREMENTS OF HOLINESS

The nineteenth chapter of Leviticus offers a succinct description of the requirements of holiness. Immediately after the admonition "Ye shall be holy," there follows the command "Ye shall fear every man his mother, and his father."

🦋 "If you wish to know," said the great Rabbi Eliezer to his disciples, "how far the honor of parents extends, then consider the example of Damah, the son of Nethina. His mother was insane and would frequently not only abuse him, but even strike him in the presence of his companions; yet would this dutiful son not suffer an ill word to escape his lips; and all that he used to say on such occasions was, 'Enough, dear mother, enough.'

"Further, one of the precious stones attached to the high priest's garments was once lost. Informed that the son of Nethina had one like it, the priests went to him and offered him a very large price for it. He consented to take the sum offered and went into an adjoining room to fetch the jewel. On entering he found his father asleep, his foot resting on the chest wherein the gem was deposited. Without disturbing his father, the son sent back to the priests and told them that he must, for the present, forego the large profit he could make, as his father was asleep.

"The case being urgent, the priests, thinking that he only said this to obtain a larger price, offered him more money. 'No,' said the dutiful son, 'I would not even for a moment disturb my father's rest, could I obtain the treasures of the world.'

"The priests waited till the father awoke, when Damah brought them the jewel. They gave him the sum they had offered the second time, but the good man refused to take it. 'I will not barter for gold the satisfaction of having done my duty. I will not make a profit out of honoring my parents. Give me what you offered at first, and I shall be satisfied.' This they did and left him with a blessing."

CHARITY

There is no Hebrew word for charity. The word that is used to denote assistance to others is zadaka, *which means "righteousness." In the ancient Temple there was a box called* Tamchui *placed in the rear. Contributions were placed in the box. At night the poor would take what they needed for their sustenance. The exemplary manner of giving is called* matan baseser, *or "giving in secret." It is held to be morally wrong to embarrass those who cannot provide for their own needs. Every man is required to assist his fellow man, thinking: "Is he not created in the image of God?" According to rabbinic law, even the pauper who receives charity must give charity.*

The commandment of Leviticus 19:9, to prohibit the reaping of the four corners of the field, is an inspiring example of God's will that we provide for the poor and the stranger.

"A man's gift maketh room for him, and bringeth him before great men" (Proverbs 18:16). Once Rabbi Eliezer and Rabbi Joshua and Rabbi Akiba went to the harbor area of Antiochia to make a collection for the support of scholars. There was a man there by the name of Abba Judan, who used to provide maintenance liberally for the needy. He subsequently became impoverished, and when he saw our rabbis there, his face turned the color of saffron.

When he came to his wife, she said to him: "Why is

your face sickly?" Said he to her: "My rabbis are here, and I do not know what to do." His wife, who was even more saintly than he, said: "We have nothing left except yon field. Go, sell half thereof, and give them the proceeds." The rabbis prayed for him, saying: "May the All-present make good your deficiency!"

After some days Abba Judan went to plow the half field he had retained; and as he was plowing, his cow fell and her leg was broken. When he went down to lift her up, the Holy One, blessed be He, gave light to his eyes, and he found a treasure there. Said he: "My cow's leg was broken, but it turned out to be for my benefit."

When our rabbis came there again, they inquired after him, saying: "How is Abba Judan doing?" They answered him: "He is Abba Judan known as the possessor of servants, Abba Judan of goats, Abba Judan of camels, Abba Judan of oxen! Who can catch a glimpse of Abba Judan?"

When the latter heard of the rabbis' presence, he went out to meet them. Said they: "How is Abba Judan doing?" Said he to them: "Your prayer has produced fruit, and fruit from the fruit." Said they to him: "As you live, even though others gave more than you did, we wrote you down at the head of the list." Then they took him and gave him a seat with themselves, and they applied to him this verse, "A man's gift maketh room for him, and bringeth him before great men."

So important was charity that Jewish tradition regarded an uncharitable man as one who incurs sin.

🦌 Rabbi Abbahu, in the name of Rabbi Eliezer, said: "We ought to be grateful to the impostors, since were it not for the impostors among the poor, then if any of them begged from a person who refused, the latter would immediately incur the penalty of death; for it says, 'And he cry unto the LORD against thee, and it be sin,' and it further says, 'The soul that sinneth, it shall die.' "

 Rabbi Johanan and Resh Lakish went down to bathe in the public baths at Tiberias. A poor man met them and said to them: "Give me alms." They replied: "When we come out we shall acquire merit through thee." When they came out they found that he was dead. They remarked: "Seeing that we did not attend to him in his lifetime, let us attend to him at his death." As they were washing him they found a bag containing six hundred denarii suspended from his neck. They exclaimed: "Blessed be He who hath chosen the wise and their words! Did not Rabbi Abbahu actually state in the name of Rabbi Eliezer: 'We ought to be grateful to the impostors'?"

 Marukba used to send money to a poor neighbor before the Day of Atonement. Once Marukba's son, who took the money, returned to his father in anger, saying: "That man was drinking old wine and so I did not give him the money."

His father replied: "Surely he must have seen better days since he has such expensive tastes. In the future I will double the amount of my gift."

 "Why was this man called Nahum Gimso?" "Because he was wont to say, whatever happened to him: 'This too [gam zeh] is for the best.' " Nahum Gimso was blind in both eyes, both his hands were crippled, his feet were both cut off, and the whole of his body was covered with leprosy. He lay stretched out in a tottering house, and his legs were thrust into pots of water, so that the ants might not be able to get to him.

One day his pupils wanted to move his bed and then the rest of the things to another house. Then he said: "My children, take the other things first and my bed last, for as long as I am here in the house you may be certain that it will not fall." They did as he told them, and no sooner had they carried the bed out than the house tumbled down.

Then his pupils said: "If you are so just a man, why do all these evil things overtake you?" "My children," he answered, "I have brought them all on myself; for one day, as I was going to the house of my father-in-law, leading with me three donkeys—one laden with provisions, one with wine, and one with rare fruits—I chanced on a poor man who stopped me and said: 'Master, give me something to eat.' 'Wait,' I said, 'until I have unladen my donkey.' But I had not ended unlading the beast before the man died. Then I went and threw myself upon him, saying: 'May my eyes, which had no pity on your eyes, lose their sight; may my hands, which had no pity on your hands, be crippled; may my feet, which had no pity on your feet, be cut off.' And my spirit was not at rest until I had said: 'May my whole body be covered with leprosy.' "

His pupils replied: "Woe to us, that we see you in this condition." But he said: "Woe to me if you were not to see me thus."

⁂ While the Hasidic rabbi Zev Wolf was on a journey, a poor young hasid came up to him and asked for financial aid. The zaddik looked in his purse, put back a large coin he happened to find, and took out a smaller one to give to the needy young man. "A young man," he said, "should not have to be ashamed of seeking assistance, but neither should he expect heaven knows what." The hasid went away with bowed head.

Rabbi Wolf called him back and asked: "Young man, what was that you were just thinking?"

"I have learned a new way to serve God," the other replied. "One should not be ashamed of receiving help, but one should not expect heaven knows what."

"That is what I meant," said the zaddik and accorded him help.

Monobaz, king of Adiabene of the first century, who embraced Judaism, was praised because in the year of great drought and scarcity, he distributed all the accumulated treasures that he owned, and the treasures accumulated by his fathers, among the people. When confronted by the members of his household with the accusation that he had squandered the wealth which his ancestors had accumulated, he replied: "My father stored up treasures below, and I am storing up treasures above. My fathers gathered treasures of money, but I have gathered treasures of souls."

Once, when our teachers went to Barbuhin to collect money for the students, they heard his son say to him, "What are we to eat today?" and he answered, "Raw vegetables," and when the son further asked whether at one bushel to the mina[2] or two to the mina, he answered, "At two to the mina, for such vegetables are withered and therefore cheap."

The rabbis thereupon said to themselves: "Why should we approach this man? Let us first do our

---

[2]The terms "mina," "denarii," and "dinars" refer to Hebrew currency.

business in the town and afterwards we will come to him."

When they had finished their business in the town they returned to him and said, "Give us a contribution." He said to them: "Go to the mistress of the house, and she will give you a bushel of denarii."

They went to his wife and said to her: "Your husband bids you give us as a contribution a bushel of dinars." She said to them: "Did he say a heaped-up bushel or just level?" They answered: "He said simply a bushel." She thereupon said: "I will give it to you heaped up, and if my husband complains, I will tell him that I have given the extra from my dowry."

The rabbis went to Barbuhin and said: "May thy Creator supply all thy needs!" He said to them: "How did my wife give it to you, heaped up or level?" They replied: "We said to her simply a bushel, and she said, 'I will give it to you heaped up, and if my husband says anything to me, I will give the extra from my dowry.' " He said to them: "In fact, it was my intention to give it you so, and why did you not approach me first of all?" They replied: "Because we heard your son say to you, 'What shall we eat today?' and you said, 'Raw vegetables,' and when he asked further, 'At one to the mina or two to the mina?' you replied, 'At two to the mina because such vegetables are dry and therefore cheap,' and we said to ourselves, 'Fancy a man with all that money eating raw vegetables at two bushels to the mina!' " He thereupon said to them: "With myself I am stingy, but with the requirements of my Creator I am not niggardly or stingy."

🐾 Once on the Great Sabbath (before the Passover) the rabbi of Roptchitz came home from the house of prayer with weary steps. "What made you so tired?" asked his wife. "It was the sermon," he replied. "I had to speak of the poor and their many needs for the coming Passover. Unleavened bread and wine and everything else is terribly high this year."

"And what did you accomplish with your sermon?" his wife asked.

"Half of what is needed," he answered. "You see, the poor are now ready to take. As for the other half, whether the rich are ready to give—I don't know about that yet."

THE EVIL OF SLANDER

The rabbis equated slander and malicious gossip with moral leprosy. Punning on the Hebrew word for talebearer, the commentators called them "peddlers," because they spread their evil merchandise from house to house and community to community. Obedience to the commandment "Thou shalt not go up and down as a talebearer" (Leviticus 19:16) was regarded as a requisite for holiness.

One day a young woman came to the rabbi of her community and confessed that she had been in the habit of telling falsehoods and spreading lies about her neighbors. She asked his help to enable her to make amends.

"Pluck a chicken," he told her, "and scatter the feathers all the way from your home to mine. Gather them up again and bring them to me and I will then give you my answer." Eagerly she promised to do this, and left. The following day she returned and said: "Rabbi, I did as you instructed me—plucked the chicken and scattered its feathers—but I regret that I couldn't bring them here, because when I tried to pick them up

I discovered the wind had blown them in all directions."

"Yes, my child," replied the rabbi sadly, "lies are like feathers; once scattered, it is impossible to retrieve them. Nor can the damage they have done ever be recalled or completely amended. Henceforth, resolve to speak the truth only."

"Who is the man that desireth life?" (Psalm 34:13).

⚜ There once was a peddler who used to go round the towns in the vicinity of Sepphoris, crying out, "Who wishes to buy the elixir of life?" and drawing great crowds around him. Rabbi Jannai, sitting and expounding in his room, heard him calling out: "Who desires the elixir of life?" The rabbi said to him: "Come here and sell it to me." The peddler said: "Neither you nor people like you require that which I have to sell."

The rabbi pressed him, and the peddler went up to him and brought out the book of Psalms and showed him the passage "Who is the man that desireth life?" What is written immediately thereafter?—"Keep thy tongue from evil. . . . Depart from evil, and do good." Rabbi Jannai said: "Solomon, too, proclaims, 'Whoso keepeth his mouth and his tongue keepeth his soul from troubles' " (Proverbs 21:23). Rabbi Jannai said: "All my life have I been reading this passage, but did not know how it was to be explained, until this hawker came and made it clear, namely, 'Who is the man that desireth life? . . . Keep thy tongue from evil, and thy lips from speaking guile' " (Psalm 34:13–14).

Thus "life and death are in the power of the tongue," say the rabbis.

A man invited some friends to dine with him and sent his servant to the market to buy the best things he could find. When dinner was served, every course consisted of tongue richly prepared with different kinds of sauce. After dinner the master angrily said to the servant, "What do you mean by bringing tongue for every course? Did I not tell you to buy the best food that could be found in the market?" The servant replied, "Have I not obeyed your orders? There is nothing better than a good tongue. It is the organ with which we speak kindness, pray to God, and spread love and friendship among men."

The next day the master sent the servant to market for some food to feed his dogs. "Get me the worst things you can find," he ordered. When the servant brought tongues again, the master cried out, "What! You dare bring tongue again!" "Most certainly," answered the slave. "There is nothing worse than a bad tongue. It is the organ that speaks lies and spreads gossip. It says mean things that make people angry with each other. There is nothing as good as a kind tongue. There is nothing as cruel as a bad one."

"Why are the fingers tapered like pegs?" ask the rabbis. "So that if one hears anything improper he can insert them in his ears."

The abuse of the gift of speech is frequently mentioned. The rabbis taught that God provided the tongue with exceptional controls.

"The Holy One, blessed be He, said to the tongue: 'All the limbs of man are erect, but you are horizontal; they are all outside the body, but you are inside. More than that, I have surrounded you with two walls, one of bone and the other of flesh.' "

HUMILITY

A man came to a Hasidic rabbi and asked that he teach him humility. At the very moment the man was speaking, the clock struck the hour.

The rabbi commented: "From the sound of the clock striking the hour, one may receive cogent instruction as to the submission of the heart. Each one of us should ask himself: 'Another hour of my life has departed; have I improved my soul within it?' "

The brevity of human life reminds us that every hour must be used for some good cause, for a worthy purpose — to advance closer to God in holiness and joy.

Standing breathless before the majesty and wonder of God, how can any human being become arrogant of heart and take undue pride in himself or his own finite achievements?

Each individual must learn to use time wisely, reverently, and, above all, with humility. He must learn to discipline himself against false pride, and thus conquer his envy and his arrogance so that he will not look down upon anyone as inferior or unworthy of his love. Are not all men God's children? Are they not created in the Divine image?

There was a king who attired himself in old garments, took up his residence in a small hut, and forbade anyone to show reverence before him. But when he honestly examined himself, the king found himself to be prouder of his seeming humility than ever before. A philosopher thereupon remarked to him: "Dress like a king; live like a king; allow the people to show due respect to you; but be humble in your inmost heart."

It is the sincere humility of heart that enables man to comprehend the infinity of God, and thus discipline his soul to worship the Holy One, blessed be He.

✍ Because of the man's pride and foolish vows, the Holy One, blessed be He, answered Jephthah by bringing him his daughter to hand (Judges 11:1 ff.). "And it came to pass, when he saw her, that he rent his clothes." But surely he could have had his vow disallowed by going to Phinehas? He thought: "I am a king! Shall I go to Phinehas?" And Phinehas argued: "I am a high priest and the son of a high priest! Shall I go to that ignoramus?" Between the two of them the poor maiden perished, and both of them incurred responsibility for her blood.

✍ A heathen once made a wager with another that he would anger the gentle Rabbi Hillel. So he went to the house of Hillel, who, next to the king, was most exalted of the Israelites. Rudely the man called out, "Where is Hillel? Where is Hillel?"

Hillel was in the act of dressing for the Sabbath. Without noticing the rudeness of the stranger, he put on his cloak and, with his usual mildness, asked him what was his pleasure. "I want to know," said the man, "why the Babylonians have round heads." "An important question, truly," answered Hillel. "The reason is because they have no experienced midwives."

The man went away, and came again in an hour, vociferating as before. The sage again said to him, "What dost thou want, my son?" "I want to know," said the man, "why the Tarmudians have weak eyes." Hillel answered, "Because they live in a sandy country; the sand flying in their eyes causes soreness."

The man, perceiving Hillel's good nature, went away disappointed. But resolving to make another effort, he came again to the rabbi. "What is thy pleasure now?" said the latter mildly. "I want to know," rejoined the former, "why the Africans have broad feet." "Because," said Hillel, "they live in a marshy land." "I fain would ask thee many more questions," said the man, "but fear thou wilt be angry." "Fear nothing," said the meek instructor of Israel; "ask as many questions as it pleases thee; and I will answer them if I can."

The man returned again and demanded: "Teach me the Torah while I stand on one foot!" Hillel said: "Do not unto others what you would not have them do unto you."

Truly astonished and fearing to lose his money, the heathen decided to insult Hillel to his face; therefore, he said, "Art thou the Hillel who is styled the prince of the Israelites?" Hillel answered in the affirmative. "Well then," said the man, "if so, may Israel not produce many like thee!" "And why?" asked the sweet-natured Hillel. "Because," replied the stranger—"because through thee I have lost four hundred zuz." "Thy money is not entirely lost," said Hillel with a smile, "because it will teach thee to be more prudent and not to make such foolish wagers. Besides, it is much better that thou lose thy money than that Hillel should lose his patience."

THE HOLINESS OF MARRIAGE

There is no word for "marriage" in the Hebrew vocabulary. The word that is used for marriage is kiddushin, *which means "holiness." This is to signify that the relationship of man and woman in marriage is not a biological union alone, or an economic partnership, but rather a sacred oneness of man and woman united through the holiness of God.*

The prophet Hosea declared that Israel had entered into a holy covenant with God, and thus wedded to holiness, became

*the bride of God. In the second chapter of his prophecy he
proclaims in the name of God:*

> I will betroth thee unto Me for ever;
> Yea, I will betroth thee unto Me in
>   righteousness, and in justice,
> And in loving-kindness, and in
>   compassion.
> And I will betroth thee unto Me in
>   faithfulness;
> And thou shalt know the LORD.

*It is through the holiness of marriage that a man and
woman may find and know God. This has been the teaching
of the rabbis through the centuries.*

Just as marriage is called kiddushin *(holiness), so the
Jewish home is called a* mikdosh m'at, *which means "a little
sanctuary." The home is regarded as sacred. It must ever be
regarded as the dwelling place of God. Therefore, the husband
officiates at the altar of his home as a high priest. The wife
assumes the role of a high priestess. The words, thoughts, and
actions of the members of the family must be in consonance
with the holiness of the home.*

*In the Jewish tradition the symbols and ceremonies, the
festivals and holy days, are "home-centered" rather than
"synagogue-centered." The festivals and holy days begin with
home observances and are to motivate a family participation in
the ritual. The family is regarded as a small society that must
be characterized by love, tenderness, justice, and peace.*

*The comparison of Israel as the bride of God is expounded in
the Midrash to teach devotion to the Torah and faith in the
Lord.*

There was a king who married a lady and made a
large settlement upon her, saying: "So many state

apartments am I preparing for you; so many fine purple garments am I giving you." The king then departed to a far country and tarried there.

When the neighbors visited this lady, they vexed her by observing: "The king has left you. He has gone away to a far country and will never return." She wept and sighed; but whenever she entered her room, she took out her settlement and read it. On seeing therein, "So many state apartments am I preparing for you; so many fine purple garments am I giving you," she was at once comforted.

At length the king returned and said to her, "My daughter, I wonder how you waited for me all these years." She answered, "My lord king, had it not been for the generous settlement which you gave me, my neighbors would long ago have caused me to perish."

Likewise, the heathen vex Israel by saying to them: "Your God has hidden His face from you and removed His *Shechinah* [Divine Presence] from your midst; He will return to you no more." They weep and sigh; but when they enter their synagogues and houses of study and read in the Torah, "And I will have respect unto you, and make you fruitful, and multiply you. . . . And I will walk among you," they are comforted.

When the era of the redemption arrives, the Holy One, blessed be He, will say to Israel: "My sons, I wonder how you waited for Me all these years"; and they will answer Him: "Lord of the universe, had it not been for Thy Torah which Thou hast given us, the heathen peoples would long ago have caused us to perish."

The Jewish wife and mother is exalted in the thirty-first chapter of Proverbs, beginning with verse 10. This passage

from scripture is read in the home during the kiddush, the
sanctification service that ushers in the Sabbath.

   Contrary to the mores and folkways of Oriental culture,
which regarded women as chattel without rights, Judaism has
ever extolled the Jewish woman as a symbol of modesty and as
the co-partner of God in the creation of life.

🦌 Rabbi Joshua of Siknim commented in Rabbi Levi's
name: "But ye have set at nought all my counsel"
(Proverbs 1:25). Thus it is written, "And the LORD built
the rib" (Genesis 2:22). This is written *wayyiben*, signi-
fying that He considered well from what part to create
her. Said He: "I will not create her from Adam's head,
lest she be light-headed or frivolous; nor from the eye,
lest she be a coquette; nor from the ear, lest she be an
eavesdropper; nor from the mouth, lest she be a gossip;
nor from the heart, lest she be prone to jealousy; nor
from the hand, lest she be light-fingered; nor from the
foot, lest she be a gadabout. But I will create her from
the modest part of man—the rib—for even when he
stands naked, that part is covered." And as He created
each limb, He ordered her, "Be a modest woman, be a
modest woman."

🦌 "And Isaac brought her into his mother Sarah's tent"
(Genesis 24:67). You find that as long as Sarah lived, a
cloud hung over her tent; when she died, that cloud
disappeared; but when Rebekah came, it returned. As
long as Sarah lived, her doors were wide open; at her
death that liberality ceased; but when Rebekah came,
that openhandedness returned. As long as Sarah lived,
there was a blessing on her dough, and the lamp used
to burn from the evening of the Sabbath until the
evening of the following Sabbath; when she died, these

ceased, but when Rebekah came, they returned. And so when he saw her following in his mother's footsteps, separating her *hallah* (Sabbath bread) in cleanness and handling her dough in cleanness, straightway "Isaac brought her into the tent."

God punishes discord severely. Although the decree of heaven does not otherwise punish anyone below twenty years of age, at Korah's rebellion (Numbers 16) the earth swallowed alive even children who were only a day old. Out of all the company of Korah and their families, only four persons escaped: On, the son of Peleth, and Korah's three sons. As it was Korah's wife who thought her inciting words plunged her husband into destruction, so to his wife did On owe his salvation. Truly to these two women applies the proverb: "Every wise woman buildeth her house: But the foolish plucketh it down with her own hands."

On, whose abilities had won him distinction, had originally joined Korah's rebellion. When he spoke of it to his wife, she said: "What benefit shalt thou reap from it? Either Moses remains master and thou art his disciple, or Korah becomes master and thou art his disciple." On saw the truth of this argument but felt he ought to keep his oath to Korah. His wife, however, gave him wine to drink which produced a deep sleep. Then, with her hair streaming, she showed herself at the door of the tent, because, she reasoned, "All the congregation are holy, and being such, they will approach no woman whose hair is uncovered." And so it was that none of Korah's company would approach the tent of On when they saw the woman thus.

When the earth opened to swallow Korah's company, On's wife seized her husband's bed and said, "O Lord of the world! My husband made a solemn vow never again to take part in the dissensions. Thou that livest and endurest to all eternity canst punish him hereafter if ever he prove false to his vow." God heard, and On was saved.

When her husband hesitated to ask Moses' forgiveness, the wife of On went to Moses in his stead. Moses heeded her story, went to On's tent, and said: "On, the son of Peleth, step forth, God will forgive thee thy sins." It is with reference to this miraculous deliverance and to his life spent in doing penance that this former follower of Korah was called On, "the penitent," son of Peleth, "miracle." His true name was Nemuel, the son of Eliab, a brother of Dathan and Abiram.

⚜ It is related of a pious man who was married to a pious woman that, being childless, they divorced each other. He went and married a wicked woman and she made him wicked. She went and married a wicked man and made him righteous. It follows that all depends upon the woman.

⚜ An emperor said to Rabbi Gamaliel, "Your God is a thief, because it is written, 'The LORD God caused a deep sleep to fall upon the man, and he slept; and He took one of his ribs" (Genesis 2:21).

The rabbi's daughter said to her father: "Permit me to answer him." She then said to the emperor: "Give me an officer to investigate a complaint." "For what purpose?" the emperor asked. She replied, "Thieves broke into our house during the night and stole a silver cup belonging to us, but left a gold one behind." "Would that such a thief visited me every day!" he exclaimed. "Was it not, then, a splendid thing for the first man when a single rib was taken from him and a woman to attend upon him was supplied in its stead!" she retorted.

A certain Roman lady put a question to Rabbi Jose, son of Halafta. She said to him: "Everybody admits that in six days God created the world. From those six days until now, however, what has He been doing?" The rabbi said to her: "He causes a change of fortune for all men, saying: 'So-and-so who was rich shall become poor, and So-and-so who was poor shall become rich'; as it is stated, 'The LORD maketh poor, and maketh rich' " (I Samuel 2:7).

Rabbi Berekiah said that Rabbi Jose did not give her this answer, but that this is what he said to her: "He arranges matrimonial unions in this world, and says: 'Such-and-such a man shall marry such-and-such a woman; and such-and-such a woman shall be married to such-and-such a man,' and He causes them to dwell in houses." She said to him: "I can arrange a thousand marriages in one day." Rabbi Jose was silent and went away.

What did she do? She brought a thousand slaves and a thousand handmaids and united them in marriage with one another. She ordered: "Such-and-such a slave shall marry So-and-so; and such-and-such a handmaid shall be married to So-and-so." As soon as they came in to their partners at night, quarreling broke out among them and they rose and beat one another. In the morning the slaves went to her, one with his head bruised, another with his hand bruised.

She sent for Rabbi Jose and told him about this incident. He said to her: "If this matter seems easy to you it is as difficult to the Omnipresent as the dividing of the Red Sea;" hence it is written: "God maketh the solitary to dwell in a house." What is the meaning of

"God maketh the solitary to dwell"? The Holy One, blessed be He, sits and judges them and brings one from one place and another from a different place and causes them to dwell in one house.

✥ A certain Israelite of Sidon, having been married above ten years without being blessed with offspring, in accordance with the tradition, determined to be divorced from his wife. With this view he brought her before Rabbi Simeon, son of Yochai. The rabbi, who was unfavorable to divorces, endeavored at first to dissuade him from it. Seeing the man disinclined, however, to accept his advice, he addressed him and his wife thus: "My children, when you were first joined in the holy bands of wedlock, were ye not rejoiced? Did ye not make a feast and entertain your friends? Now, since ye are resolved to be divorced, let your separation be like your union. Go home, make a feast, entertain your friends, and on the morrow come to me, and I will comply with your wishes."

So reasonable a request, and coming from such authority, could not be rejected. They accordingly went home and prepared a sumptuous entertainment to which they invited their friends. During the hours of merriment the husband, being elated with wine, thus addressed his wife: "My beloved, we have lived together happily these many, many years; it is only the want of children which makes me wish for a separation. To convince thee, however, that I bear thee no ill will, I give thee permission to take with thee out of my house anything thou likest best." "Be it so," rejoined the woman.

The cup went round and the people were merry; having drunk rather freely, most of the guests fell asleep, among them the master of the feast. The lady no

sooner perceived it than she ordered him to be carried
to her father's house and to be put into a bed prepared
for the purpose.

The fumes of the wine having gradually evaporated,
the man awoke. Finding himself in a strange place, he
wondered and exclaimed, "Where am I? How came I
here? What means all this?" His wife, who had waited
to see the issue of her stratagem, stepped from behind
a curtain, and begging him not to be alarmed, told him
that he was now in her father's house.

"In thy father's house!" exclaimed the still astonished
husband; "how should I come in thy father's house?"
"Be patient, my dear husband," replied the prudent
woman; "be patient, and I will tell thee all. Recollect,
didst thou not tell me last night that I might take out of
thy house whatever I valued most? Now believe me,
my beloved, among all thy treasures there is not one I
value so much as I do thee; nay, there is not a treasure
in this world I esteem so much as I do thee."

The husband, overcome by so much kindness, embraced her, was reconciled to her, and they lived
thenceforth very happily together.

*In a humorous story the rabbis attempted to discourage
polygamy, especially in the case where a man takes two wives,
one young and the other old.*

🦌 An elderly man took unto himself two wives—one
young and the other old. During the night the young
wife plucked out his gray hairs so he would appear
young. The older wife plucked out his black hairs so
that he would appear old. Between the two of them, the
man became bald.

*It is not humor, but holiness, that characterizes the Jewish
concept of marriage. The rabbis were not inhibited in dis-*

cussing birth control and the physical aspects of marriage.
They recognized the importance of sex in marriage but refused
to make sex the totality of marriage.

🦎 "Why does it say in Genesis: 'Be fruitful, and multiply?' It is redundant. Wouldn't it have been enough to
say, 'Be fruitful'? — or wouldn't it have been enough to
say, 'multiply'? Why add something to the text?" They
answered: "This is to show that there must be a plus to
marriage. Animals copulate and multiply. In marriage
there must be more than a physical relationship. A
husband and wife must bring love, tenderness, and
holiness not only to the sexual act, but to their marriage
vows."

🦎 Rabbi Gamaliel gave his daughter in marriage. "Father," she requested, "pray for me." "May you never
return hither," said he to her. When she gave birth to a
son she again begged him, "Father, give me your
blessing." "May 'woe' never leave your mouth," replied
he. "Father," she exclaimed, "on both occasions of my
rejoicing you have cursed me!" "Both were blessings,"
he replied. "Living at peace in your home, you will not
return here, and as long as your son lives, 'woe' will not
leave your mouth: 'Woe that my son has not eaten!'
'Woe that he has not drunk!' 'Woe that he has not gone
to school!' "

Commenting on the scriptural verse "It is not good that the
man should be alone," the rabbis offered this touching homily:

🦎 Once, men and women were joined together as one
(very much like Siamese twins). They incurred the
wrath of God, and therefore He sent an angel with a
sword to cut them asunder, and cast them through time

and space. A heavenly voice said: "Now you must go forth to seek your true mate through all eternity. When you find your true mate, you find yourself. When you find your counterpart, then you will be complete. Until you do, you are only half. It is only when you find your mate that you are joined together again as one: one flesh, one heart, and one soul."

LOVE THE STRANGER

As the nineteenth chapter of Leviticus comes to a conclusion, the scripture states: "The stranger that sojourneth with you shall be unto you as the homeborn among you, and thou shalt love him as thyself; for ye were strangers in the land of Egypt: I am the Lord." It is difficult enough to love thy neighbor as thyself. How much more, then, is it difficult to love the stranger as thyself?

When Abraham sat at his tent door according to his custom, waiting to entertain strangers, he saw an old man, weary with age and travel, coming toward him. Abraham received him kindly, washed his feet, caused him to sit down, and provided supper. When Abraham observed that the old man ate without a prayer or blessing, he asked him why he did not worship the God in heaven. The old man told him that he worshiped fire only and acknowledged no other God. When Abraham heard this he became angry and forced the old man out of his tent into the night.

When the old man had departed, God called to Abraham and asked where the stranger was. Abraham replied: "I thrust him away because he did not worship Thee." God answered: "I have suffered him these eighty years although he dishonored Me, and couldst thou not endure him one night?" Abraham rushed out into the night, overtook the stranger, and brought him back into his tent, where he accorded him hospitality and wise instruction.

HOLINESS IN PRACTICAL AFFAIRS

⚘ Rabbi Huna once asked his son Raba why he did not attend the lectures of Rabbi Hisda, who spoke on medical subjects. "Because," replied the son, "he treats only of temporal and worldly concerns." "What!" said the father. "He occupies himself with that which is necessary for the preservation of human beings—and this you call worldly affairs! Trust me, this is among the most estimable of studies."

On the verse "that ye may remember and do all My commandments, and be holy unto your God" (Numbers 15:40), the rabbis offered the following parable:

⚘ A man fell into the sea. The captain of the boat threw him a rope and said, "Cling to this rope and do not let go of it; if you loosen your hold upon it you will drown!" Similarly said the Holy One, blessed be He: "So long as ye cleave to the commandments, 'ye cleave unto the LORD your God and are alive every one of you this day' " (Deuteronomy 4:4); and it is also said, "Take fast hold of instruction, let her not go; keep her, for she is thy life" (Proverbs 4:13). "And be holy"—so long as you fulfill the commandments you are rendered holy.

This exemplifies the rabbinic insistence that holiness is not mystical and otherworldly, but is derived from obedience to God's commandments as revealed in the Torah. The nine-

teenth chapter of Leviticus, called the Holiness Code, attests to the moral and ethical nature of holiness. The authority for ethical conduct bears the imprimatur of divinity. Each commandment is supported by the declaration: "I am the LORD." If man truly wishes to achieve holiness, let him obey God and serve Him by deeds of loving-kindness and justice in behalf of God's children.

Chapter V

JUSTICE

"How can there be holiness without social justice?" ask the rabbis. They remind us that the Holiness Code (Leviticus 19) is replete with God's commandments requiring justice in man's dealings with his fellow man:

🕉 Thou shalt not oppress they neighbor, nor rob him; the wages of a hired servant shall not abide with thee all night until the morning. Thou shalt not curse the deaf, nor put a stumbling-block before the blind, but thou shalt fear thy God: I am the Lord. Ye shall do no unrighteousness in judgment: thou shalt not respect the person of the poor [discriminating in his behalf because he is poor], nor favor the person of the mighty; but in righteousness shalt thou judge thy neighbor (Leviticus 19:13–16).

In commenting on the verse "Thou shalt not curse the deaf," the rabbis correctly inquire:

🦋 "Why? Since the deaf cannot hear the curse, what is so reprehensible?" They answered: "Thou shalt not curse the deaf because even a deaf man is created in the Divine image. Even though he is unable to hear, when you curse him, you are also cursing the Divine image."

GOD IS EXALTED THROUGH JUSTICE

🦋 "Of all that I have created I love only justice," as it is said, "For I the LORD love justice" (Isaiah 61:8). God said to Israel: "My children, by your life, as a result of your respecting justice, I am exalted." Whence this? As it is said, "But the LORD of hosts is exalted through justice" (Isaiah 5:16). "And because you exalt Me through justice I too will act righteously and will cause My holiness to dwell amongst you." Whence this? As it is said, "And God the Holy One is sanctified through righteousness" (Isaiah 5:16). "And if you will respect both righteousness and justice I will immediately redeem you with a complete redemption." Whence this? As it is said, "Thus saith the LORD: Keep ye justice, and do righteousness; for My salvation is near to come, and My favor to be revealed" (Isaiah 56:1).

🦋 Rabbi Wolf's wife had a quarrel with her maidservant. She accused the girl of breaking a bowl and wanted payment for it. The girl, on the other hand, denied breaking the article and refused to replace it. The quarrel became more and more heated. At last the wife of Rabbi Wolf decided to refer the matter to the court of arbitration of the Torah, and quickly dressed for a visit to the *rav* (judge). When Rabbi Wolf saw this, he too put on his Sabbath clothes. When his wife inquired the reason, he told her that he planned to accompany her. She objected that this was not fitting for him, and that besides she knew quite well what to say to the judge. "You know it quite well," the rabbi replied. "But the poor orphan, your maidservant, in whose behalf I am coming, does not know it, and who except me is there to defend her cause?"

⁂ One night thieves entered Rabbi Wolf's house and began to take whatever they happened to find. From his room the rabbi watched them but did nothing to stop them. Finally they took some utensils, including a jug from which a sick man had drunk that same evening. Rabbi Wolf ran after them. "My children," he said, "whatever you have found here, I beg you to regard as gifts from me. I do not at all begrudge them. But please do not take the jug! The breath of a sick man is clinging to it, and you are in danger of catching his disease!"

From this time on, the rabbi said every night before going to bed: "All my possessions are common property." This he did, so that if thieves came again, they would not be guilty of theft.

⁂ The rabbis asked: "What does scripture mean when it commands, 'Justice, justice shall ye pursue'? Why is the word 'justice' repeated? Wouldn't it have been enough to state, 'Justice shall ye pursue'?" "No," they answered, "every word of scripture has religious meaning, even when it appears to be redundant."

Scripture commands, "Justice, justice shall ye pursue," in order to teach that justice must apply to the Jew and non-Jew, to the homeborn and the stranger, to the rich and the poor, to the wise and the simple, to the righteous and the wicked.

Some sages would add "justice even to animals." Rabbi Judah said: "A man is forbidden to eat anything until he has fed his beast." Rabbi Tanhuma ben Abba cited Proverbs 11:30, "He that is wise winneth souls." The rabbis said: "This refers to Noah, for in the ark he fed and sustained the animals with much care. He gave to each animal its special food and fed each at its proper period, some in the daytime and some at night. Thus he gave chopped straw to the camel, barley to the ass, and vine tendrils to the elephant. So for twelve months he did not sleep by night or day, because all the time he was busy feeding the animals."

🥦 "And the LORD hath chosen thee to be His own treasure" (Deuteronomy 14:2). Said Rabbi Eliezer, son of Rabbi Jose ben Zimri: "In the case of the sacrifices, also, it is so. The Holy One, blessed be He, said: 'The ox is pursued by the lion, the goat is pursued by the leopard, the lamb by the wolf; do not offer unto Me, from those that pursue but from those that are pursued.' Hence it is written, 'When a bullock, or a sheep, or a goat, is brought forth . . . it may be accepted for an offering.' "

Ancient Jewish law did not permit predatory animals to be used as sacrifices on the altar of God. Any animal that subsisted on others or was a beast or bird of prey was not only prohibited as food, but was likewise rejected as a proper sacrifice. This was to teach the people that cruel and predatory actions are not acceptable to God.

🥦 A woodsman went into the forest to ask the trees to give him wood for an ax. It seemed so modest a request that the principal trees at once agreed to it, and it was settled among them that the plain, unpretentious ash should furnish what was wanted.

No sooner had the woodsman fitted the staff to his purpose than he began laying about him on all sides, felling the noblest trees in the forest. The oak whispered to the cedar: "Our first concession has lost us all. If we had not sacrificed our humblest neighbor, we ourselves might have stood for ages."

How aptly and how tragically this midrash may be applied to international relations. The phenomenon of larger nations sacrificing smaller nations to an aggressor, only to be cut down as the next victims, has been demonstrated in contemporary history.

This may also be applied to those who would yield the rights and welfare of minority groups to hate-mongers. Ultimately, even the majority groups find their own rights and welfare in jeopardy. Prejudice and hatred need no passports to advance from one group to another.

This is reminiscent of a Midrashic commentary on the biblical verse that refers to Israel as a "scattered lamb." They tell us that if a lamb is suspended upon a hook and one part of the body is struck, another part trembles. So it is, they say, that when Jews are attacked in Rome, Jews in Caesarea tremble. They did not limit their homily, however, to those of the Jewish faith but attempted to teach that when one religion or race is attacked, the others may well tremble.

Alexander the Great marched away to a province named Africa. The people came out to meet him with golden apples, golden pomegranates, and golden bread. "What is the meaning of this?" he cried. "Do they eat gold in your country?" They answered him: "Is it not so in your country?" He said to them: "It is not your possessions I have come to see but your laws."

As Alexander sat observing in their court, two men came before the king for judgment. One said: "Your majesty! I bought a carob tree from this man, and in scooping it out I found a treasure therein, so I said to him: 'Take your treasure, for I bought the carob tree but not the treasure.' " The other argued: "Just as you are afraid of risking punishment for robbery, so am I. When I effected the sale I sold you the carob tree and all that is therein." The king called one of them and said to him: "Have you a son?" "Yes," he replied. He called the other and asked him: "Have you a daughter?" "Yes," he replied. "Go," said the king to them, "and let them get married to each other, and let them both enjoy the treasure."

Alexander of Macedon began to show surprise. "Why," the king asked him, "are you surprised? Have I not judged well?" "Yes," Alexander assured him. "If this case had arisen in your country," the king asked, "what would you have done?" Alexander replied: "We should have removed this man's head and that one's, and the treasure would have gone to the king."

"Does the sun," the king asked Alexander, "shine in your country?" "Yes," he replied. "Perhaps," said the other, "there are small cattle in your country?" "Yes," he answered. The king exclaimed: "Oh, woe to that man! It is not because of you but because of the merit of the small cattle that the sun shines upon you and the rain falls upon you. For the sake of the small cattle you are saved!"

The fair and just distribution of the contributions of the earth was regarded as the will of God. Man should never arrogate to himself the belief that he can really possess the earth.

🦌 Once two disputants came before Rabbi Ezekiel Laudau. Both claimed ownership of a tract of land. After listening to their arguments, Ezekiel Laudau said, "Take me to the land." They took him to the disputed land. He said, "Let the earth itself render judgment." To the amazement of the two disputants, he placed his ear to the ground and listened. After a few moments he stood up and announced: "The earth has rendered its decision: 'I belong to neither of you, but both of you belong to me.' "

THE DIGNITY OF LABOR

The nineteenth chapter of Leviticus, the Holiness Code, does not conclude with the admonition to observe ritual or withdraw from the affairs of the world. Quite to the contrary, it deals with practical aspects of life and the application of justice in business:

> Ye shall do no unrighteousness in judgment, in meteyard, in weight, or in measure. Just balances, just weights, a just ephah, and a just hin, shall ye have: I am the LORD your God, who brought you out of the land of Egypt. And ye shall observe all My statutes, and all Mine ordinances, and *do* them: I am the LORD (Leviticus 19:35–37).

The rabbis whose wisdom exalts the Talmud and Midrash engaged in ordinary pursuits of labor to provide sustenance for themselves and their families. In those days rabbis did not receive salaries from the congregation or the community. Rabbi Akiba collected bundles of wood and sold them. Rabbi Joshua was a charcoal burner. Rabbi Meir was a scribe. Rabbi Jose ben Chalaphta was a worker in leather. Rabbi Jochanan made sandals. Rabbi Judah was a baker, and Rabbi Abba Saul was a kneader of dough. They were firmly convinced of the dignity of honest labor.

At the time the Holy One, blessed be He, informed Adam, "Thorns also and thistles shall the earth bring forth to thee" (Genesis 3:18), his eyes filled up with tears. Adam said to God: "Sovereign of the universe, am I and my donkey to feed in the same manger?" But when God added, "In the sweat of thy face shalt thou eat bread," he immediately became calm. That teaches us that through his labor, man raises himself above the rest of the animal kingdom.

The employer must ever be considerate of the rights of labor. He must obey the command set forth in Leviticus 19:13: "The wages of a hired servant shall not abide with thee all night until the morning." The poor man may need the money to feed himself and his family that very night. Biblical law also ordains that if a man asks for a loan and his cloak is given as a pledge, whether he returns the loan or not, his cloak must be returned to him by nightfall because that may be his only covering from the cold.

The porters engaged by Rabba Bar-Chanak broke a cask of wine belonging to him, and as a penalty he took their coats from them. They went to the sage and complained. The sage thereupon ordered Rabba to restore the garments. "Is that the law?" Rabba asked. The sage replied: "It is written, 'that thou mayest walk in the way of good men' " (Proverbs 2:20). He gave them back their coats. The laborers then said: "We are poor and have toiled through the day and are hungry; we are in great need." The sage said to Rabba, "Go and pay their wages." Rabba asked, "Is that the law?" He replied, "Yes, for it is written, 'and keep the paths of the righteous' " (Proverbs 2:20).

It has been unfairly contended that the stringency of Jewish law controverts kindness and the spirit of justice. This is manifestly untrue. As the above story indicates, the law is to be used for the promotion of kindness, justice, mercy, and truth. It was to protect the weak, grant justice to the oppressed, and as its name (Halacha—"to walk") implies, cause men to walk in the ways of the living God.

Every man must labor diligently at his work. Laziness is offensive to God.

King Solomon summoned two skilled craftsmen and ordered each to build a room of unequaled magnificence. They could request any material no matter how costly, and it would be given to them. The king warned: "At the end of six months, the work must be completed! I personally will examine the results of your labors." If their efforts met with his approval, there would be a generous reward; if not, the penalty would be death.

One of the workmen, who was diligent, began at once to requisition costly materials, precious jewels, and delicately woven fabrics. The other, who was lazy, assured himself that he had sufficient time and need not exert himself unduly.

Two months passed, and the industrious workman had made considerable progress in building his room. But the lazy workman had not even started. By the end of the fifth month the work of the former was nearing completion. He now had an additional month to perfect the room to his satisfaction.

The lazy workman, who had not even started, now realized that he had but one month to work. Dismay and panic seized his heart as he remembered Solomon's warning. Looking at the nearly completed room of his fellow workman, he was awed by its workmanship and indescribable beauty. What could he do? He gave himself up for lost until he conceived of a plan to deceive Solomon, save his own life, and at the same time merit a generous reward.

Since his room was to be adjacent to the room of the diligent artisan, he requisitioned nothing but mirrors. With the mirrors carefully placed on the walls and ceiling, his room reflected the magnificence of the adjoining room. A quick glance would reveal two identical rooms. Satisfied that his hoax would be effective, he confidently awaited the inspection of the king.

Shortly thereafter, Solomon came to view the results. He first entered the room of the diligent workman and was enthralled with its magnificence. Then he turned to the work of the lazy artisan and was amazed to behold a room of equal beauty and magnificence. Nodding to both workmen, he summoned them to appear at the palace to receive their reward.

Considerably relieved, the lazy workman gloated at having so easily deceived the wise Solomon. Grateful that God had granted him the health and the skill to complete his work, the diligent workman breathed a silent prayer of gratitude.

At the palace the king ordered his servants to place a large bag of gold upon the table, and to the industrious workman he announced, "This is your reward." The latter gratefully accepted the gold and returned to his family.

The lazy workman struggled to conceal his satisfaction as Solomon placed another large bag of gold upon the table. As the artisan stepped forward to claim his reward, the king commanded, "Wait!" The startled workman stopped as Solomon placed a mirror next to the bag of gold. Pointing to the reflection in the mirror, Solomon turned to the workman and said, "This is your reward." The lazy workman returned to his family empty-handed, in disgrace and dishonor.

This story from the Jewish homiletical tradition has been interpreted in many ways. The obvious meaning is that we get out of life what we put into it. Another interpretation is that the King of all Kings has summoned each of us for His work. We are given a limited time to complete our assignments. We may work faithfully or we may attempt to deceive the Sovereign of the universe. Ultimately we are summoned on the day of reckoning. If we have worked earnestly, we will receive a reward for our labors. If we have been remiss, then we will receive nothing but disappointing reflections of the reward of God.

One may also consider this story in the sense of working for our faith. We must work for more than reflections of piety, justice, brotherhood, and peace. It is only through honest and devoted effort that we will succeed in building God's kingdom on earth.

Frequently this story is interpreted to mean that the laboring man must give his best efforts to his employer and must feel a moral obligation to earn the wages that are paid to him.

THE RIGHTS OF MANAGEMENT

The Talmud did not forget that the employer also has rights. The rabbis taught that a workman must be faithful in his labor, and not cheat his employer in any way. He must always give his employer his best efforts. To do otherwise is to defraud him of his money.

🕱 The opinion of Abba Joseph, the builder, was sought on a certain matter. He was found standing upon some scaffolding. The questioner said to him, "I want to ask you something." But his answer was, "I can't come down because I am hired by the day."

Two scholars went to him to ask that he should pray for rain. They did not find him at his house. They proceeded to the field and saw him plowing the ground. They greeted him cordially, but he took no notice of them and never halted his plowing. When he returned home he found the two rabbis waiting for him. They asked him why he had ignored their greeting. He replied: "I hired myself out for the day, and I was of the opinion that I had no right to interrupt my work and thus cheat my employer."

GOD'S JUSTICE

The problem that has confronted man ever since the dawn of human thought is related to the ubiquitous question, how do we reconcile God's justice with the existence of suffering and evil? Theologians call this the problem of theodicy. Abraham, in pleading for the evil inhabitants of Sodom and Gomorrah, asked: "Shall not the Judge of all the earth do justly?" (Genesis 18:25). The entire book of Job wrestles with the problem of reconciling suffering and evil with the mercy and justice of God.

Rabbinic teaching insists that the finite is not able to fully grasp or comprehend the infinite. How can mortal man presume to question the wisdom or the justice of the Eternal

God? Even though we cannot understand, we must praise
God in suffering and in sorrow with the faith that what God
does is for the best.

Rabbi Akiba once traveled forth accompanied by a
rooster, a lamp, and a donkey. At nightfall he arrived at
a village and asked for hospitality. The people drove
him away with curses and blows. Rabbi Akiba said,
"God means this for good," and wearily proceeded into
the forest to spend the night. Making himself comfortable he ate a morsel of bread, but was startled to hear
the frenzied squawking of the rooster. He jumped
quickly to his feet and saw a fox running away with the
unfortunate rooster. Rabbi Akiba said, "God means this
for good," and settled himself to study by the light of
the lamp. A wind came up and blew out the light. The
rabbi said, "God means this for good." He noticed that
the donkey had strayed away. Anxiously he looked for
it this way and that, until he gave the animal up for lost.
Now, in the morning, he would have to walk the long
distance to his destination. Akiba sighed as he said,
"God means this for good."

The next morning he proceeded to his destination on
foot. Having completed his mission, he returned homeward. When he reached the village whose inhabitants
had treated him in such a cruel fashion, he noted to his
amazement that not a single person was alive. Robbers
had entered the town the very night he had sought
hospitality, robbed the town, and mercilessly killed the
inhabitants.

When he realized this, Akiba said: "Who can discern
the wisdom of God? If the villagers had permitted me to
remain, I would have been massacred with the rest.
Since the brigands' tracks lead from the forest, if the
rooster had crowed or the donkey brayed, or if they had

seen the light of my lamp, I would surely have been destroyed. In truth, one should rely upon the judgment of God."

🦂 Once Elijah granted his friend Rabbi Joshua ben Levi the fulfillment of any wish he might express. All the rabbi asked was that he might accompany Elijah on his wanderings through the world. Elijah consented, but insisted that, however odd the rabbi might think Elijah's actions, he was not to ask for an explanation. If ever he demanded why, they would have to part company.

Elijah and the rabbi journeyed together until they reached the house of a poor man whose only earthly possession was a cow. The man and his wife invited the strangers into their house, set before them food and drink, and made up a comfortable couch for them. When Elijah and the rabbi departed on the following day, Elijah prayed that the man's cow might die. Before they left the house, the animal had expired. Rabbi Joshua, shocked by the misfortune, thought: "Is that to be the poor man's reward for all his kind services to us?"

That night they reached the house of a wealthy man. Though they passed the night under his roof, he neither greeted them nor offered them food and drink. This rich man wanted a wall repaired that had tumbled down. When Elijah left the house, he prayed that the wall might erect itself, and lo, it stood upright. Rabbi Joshua was amazed but he made no comment.

The two traveled on again until they reached an ornate synagogue. The worshipers, however, did not correspond in character to the magnificence of the building, for when it came to satisfying the needs of the pilgrims, they were most ungenerous. As they were leaving, Elijah wished for those present that God might raise them all to be leaders. Rabbi Joshua again said nothing.

In the next town they were cordially received. For these kind hosts Elijah, on leaving, wished that God might give them but a single leader. Now the rabbi could not restrain himself; he demanded an explanation of Elijah's freakish actions.

As they separated, Elijah spoke thus: "The poor man's cow was killed because the death of his wife had been ordained in heaven, and I prayed that the man's property be taken instead of his wife. As for the rich man, there was a treasure beneath the dilapidated wall; hence I set up the wall miraculously in order to prevent his finding the gold. I wished that the inhospitable people in the synagogue might have many heads, for a place of numerous leaders is bound to be ruined by disputes. To our gracious hosts, however, I wished for a single head, for with one to guide a town, success will attend all its undertakings. Know, then, that if thou seest an evildoer prosper, it is not always unto his advantage, and if a righteous man suffers distress, think not God is unjust."

With or without man's knowledge, God's law of retribution applies to the affairs of men. Goodness is rewarded and evil is punished even though it may not be at the time or in the way we would expect.

The Roman conqueror Titus, after his successful conquest of Judea, desecrated the Temple, using it for a brothel. He took his sword and cut asunder the curtain of the Holy Ark, exclaiming, "I am stronger than the God of Israel!" God decided to destroy Titus by the smallest of His creation.

As he was leaving the bath, the attendants of Titus mixed for him a vial of *poterion* and wine. The Holy One, blessed be He, arranged that there should be in the goblet a gnat, which entered Titus's nose and reached his brain. It began piercing his brain, devouring it, and growing in size as it changed into a young dove. Titus ordered, "Summon the physicians to split my brain open, so that I may know with what the God of this people has punished me." They summoned the physicians, who split his brain open and found a kind of young dove weighing two pounds.

Rabbi Eleazar ben R. Jose said: "I was in Rome at the time, and they placed the young dove on one scale and two pounds on the other, and they balanced. They set it in a dish, and as it altered, so did he alter. When the dove changed back into a gnat and flew away, the soul of Titus flew to destruction and everlasting abhorrence."

So it is with prejudice. The rabbis taught, "Pity the persecutor," because through his prejudice he sows the seeds of his own destruction. Therefore they said, "Rather be of the persecuted than a persecutor."

Rabbi Hiyya ben Abba said: "To what can the heathen be compared? To one who hated the king and sought to master him, but could not. So what did he do? He went to the king's statue and was about to cast it down, when fear of the king seized him lest he should be slain for this treason. He therefore took an iron implement with which to undermine the wall, thinking to himself: 'Once I overthrow the foundations, the statue is bound to topple down.' In like manner do the heathen come to provoke God, but finding that they cannot do so, they attack Israel instead."

This is consistent with modern dynamic psychology, which refers to "transference" as a common phenomenon. Frequently one transfers hatred or prejudice from one person or institution to another. Freud suggests that an atheist may have a hatred of his own father. He transfers the hatred to his Heavenly Father.

🦁 A Jew passed in front of the Roman Emperor Hadrian and greeted him. The emperor asked, "Who are you?" He answered, "I am a Jew." The emperor exclaimed, "Dare a Jew pass in front of Hadrian and greet him!" He ordered, "Take him and cut off his head."

Another Jew passed, and seeing what had happened to the first man, did not greet the emperor. Hadrian asked, "Who are you?" He answered, "A Jew." The emperor exclaimed, "Dare a Jew pass in front of Hadrian without giving greeting! Take him out and cut off his head."

His senators said to Hadrian: "We cannot understand your actions. He who greeted you was killed, and he who did not greet you was killed!" He replied to them: "Do you seek to advise me how I wish to kill those I hate! No matter what they do I shall seek means to destroy them." And the Holy Spirit cried out and said, "Thou hast seen all their vengeance and all their devices against me" (Lamentations 3:60).

Through his hatred Hadrian brought evil to himself and to his countrymen. Prejudice is irrational and portends the weakness of character that results in self-destruction. Hatred is a poison that reacts as violently on the poisoner as on the poisoned.

Just as a violation of the physical laws of the universe will result in punishment, so when man violates God's moral laws, he suffers the inevitable consequence of his actions.

🐾 There was once a governor who used to put to death the receivers and release the thieves, and all used to find fault with him, saying that he was not acting correctly. What did he do? He issued a proclamation throughout the province, saying: "Let all the people go out to the campus!" What did he do then? He brought some weasels and placed before them portions of food. The weasels took the portions and carried them to their holes. The next day he again issued a proclamation, saying: "Let all the people go out to the campus!" Again he brought weasels and placed portions of food before them, but stopped up all the holes. The weasels took the portions and carried them to their holes, but finding these stopped up, they brought their portions back to their places. He did this to demonstrate that all the trouble is due to receivers.

Frequently we blame the criminals and corrupt politicians for the evil in our society. We berate those who publish scandal magazines and castigate those who sponsor suggestive advertising and questionable motion pictures. The Midrash suggests that those who support evil contribute to injustice and immorality.

THE SUFFERING OF THE RIGHTEOUS

We can understand why the evil may suffer, but what purpose is there to the suffering of the just and the innocent?

🐾 Rabbi Jonathan, commenting on the text "The Lord trieth the righteous" (Psalm 11:5), said: "The potter does not test cracked vessels. It is useless to tap them even once, because they would break. He does, however, test the good ones, because no matter how many times he taps them they do not break. Even so God tests not the wicked but the righteous."

꙰ The rabbis taught that Israel may be compared to the oil of an olive for three reasons. First, in order for an olive to yield its essence, its pure oil, it must be subjected to pressure and crushed. History records that the Jews made their greatest contributions to religion, to art, to science at times of persecution and suffering.

Rabbi Moshe, the son of the maggid of Koznitz, said: "It is written: 'Pure olive oil beaten for the light.' We are to be beaten and bruised, but in order to glow with light."

The second reason that Israel is compared to an olive is this: Take the oil of an olive and put it in a glass of water. The oil will not mix with the water but remains apart. So even at a time of suffering, Israel, like the oil, must not mix with evil, hatred, prejudice, or irreverence, but must remain separate and apart.

The third reason is this: If we take the oil of an olive and attempt to keep it at the bottom of a glass of water, the oil will rise to the top. So it is when Israel is crushed low and forced into the gutters of human degradation by oppression. Then those of the Jewish faith must rise above their suffering, rise above injustice, upward, in the direction of God.

꙰ "Why is Israel compared to the sand?" ask the rabbis. An interpretation of the verse "as the sand of the sea" is given. What is the nature of sand? If it is put into the fire it comes out as glass from which utensils are made.

Thus Israel, when subjected to fire, must emerge as glass to serve as utensils for the work of God.

At a time of great tribulation for Israel, the Hasidic

rabbi Elimelekh brooded more and more. He began to
doubt the validity of God's justice. Then his dead
teacher, the sage of Mezritch, appeared to him in a
dream. Rabbi Elimelekh cried out: "Why are you silent
in such dreadful need?" The sage answered: "In heaven
we see that all that seems evil to you is a work of
mercy."

SENSITIVITY TO ONE'S FELLOW MAN

*The duty to act justly is derived from the requirement to be
just because justice is an attribute of God. Justice is also
predicated upon the sanctity of man created in the Divine
image. To ignore those who "cry out of the depths" for help is
to ignore the cry and supplications of God.*

*To enlarge his capacity for God and thus increase his
spiritual potential, man must sensitize himself to the needs
and the suffering of his fellow man. Such empathy leads to a
more acute perception of justice.*

*Rabbi Johanan gave it as his own opinion: "Any distress
shared by Israel and the nations of the world is a real distress,
but any distress confined to Israel is not such a distress."*

*A Sanhedrin which executed a person once in seven years
was called destructive. Rabbi Eleazar ben Azariah said, "Once
in seventy years." Rabbi Tarphon and Rabbi Akiba said: "If we
were members of the Sanhedrin, never would a person be put
to death."*

🦌 "And Moses cried unto the Lord" (Numbers 12:13).
Moses can be compared to a warrior who once had a
chain of punishment around his neck of which he was
later freed. Subsequently he observed the chain placed
on the neck of another, and he began to cry. On being
asked: "Why do you cry?" he replied, "You indeed do

not know, but I know what suffering it causes lying there, for once the chain was on my neck and I know what pain it gave me." So when Moses was crying, God asked him, "Why do you cry?" He answered: "Master of the universe, I know what pain my sister is suffering for having castigated me for marrying a Cushite. Thinking of her, I remember the chain in which my hand was once placed." Whence this? As it is said, "Behold, his hand was leprous, as white as snow" (Exodus 4:6). After Moses had prayed on her behalf, God healed her. Whence this? For it is said, "And the people journeyed not till Miriam was brought in again" (Numbers 12:15). Therefore be mindful of what befell Miriam because of slander.

✄ Rabbi Joshua ben Levi said: "When Moses our teacher heard this [referring to the suffering of the children of Israel], he exclaimed before God: 'Master of the universe, let Moses and a hundred like him perish rather than that the fingernail of even one Israelite should be injured.' "

✄ Moses Leib, the Hasidic rabbi of Sassov, declared to his disciples: "I learned how we must truly love our neighbor from the conversation between two villagers which I overheard. The first said: 'Tell me, friend Ivan, do you love me?' The second: 'I love you deeply.' The first: 'Do you know, my friend, what gives me pain?' The second: 'How can I, pray, know what gives you pain?' The first: 'If you do not know what gives me pain, how can you say that you truly love me?' Understand then, my sons, to love—truly to love—means to know what brings pain to your fellow human being."

✄ Whenever the rabbi of Sassov saw anyone's suffering, either of spirit or of body, he shared it so earnestly that the other's suffering became his own. Once someone expressed his astonishment at this capacity to share in another's troubles.

"What do you mean 'share'?" said the rabbi. "It is my own sorrow; how can I help but suffer it?"

FREEDOM

The rabbis taught that there can be no justice without freedom and peace.

Rabbi Hanokh said: "The real exile of Israel in Egypt was that they had learned to endure it."

The Jewish festival of Passover is dedicated to the principle of freedom. Channukah, the Feast of Lights, commemorates the heroism of the Maccabees, who resisted the invading army of the Syrians and fought for religious freedom.

While the first commandment in the Christian tradition begins, "Thou shalt have no other gods before Me," in the Jewish tradition this is regarded as the second commandment and not the first. What then is the first commandment according to Exodus 20 and Deuteronomy 5? It is: "I am the LORD thy God, who brought thee out of the land of Egypt, out of the house of bondage."

God introduces Himself as the God of freedom. Wherein is the commandment? The commandment is implied: "Thou shalt be free!" Since God is a God of freedom, man must imitate the Divine attribute by dedicating himself to freedom. Without freedom, how can man obey the ten commandments? Freedom is a prerequisite for a moral society. Without freedom, man is not at liberty to choose the good and to reject the evil. One of the most precious gifts of God is freedom of will and the right to make moral choices.

🦌 Rabbi Jochanan ben Zakkai taught: "When a slave says, 'I love my master, my wife, and my children; I will not go out free,' then his master shall bring him to the door or the doorpost and shall bore his ear through with an awl and he shall serve for life" (Exodus 21:5–6).

Why was the ear singled out from all other limbs of the body? The Holy One, blessed be He, said: "This ear which heard My voice on Mount Sinai when I proclaimed, 'For unto Me the children of Israel are servants; they are My servants' [Leviticus 25:55], and not servants of servants, and yet this man went and acquired a master for himself that his ear be bored."

PEACE

"Sholom" (peace) is the greeting of the Jew. "Sholom" (peace) is his way of saying farewell. Without peace, how can man practice justice? Without peace how can man enter into copartnership with God in the building of His kingdom?

To bring peace between men, between husband and wife, and between nations has ever been regarded as an exalted objective of the Jewish faith.

🦌 Once when Rabbi Yannai was taking a walk he encountered a young man who was dressed like a student, so he invited the youth to his house. He tried to engage him in learned discourse during the meal, first on the scriptures, and then on the Mishna, the Midrash, and the Talmud, but found the guest ignorant on all these subjects. Finally the rabbi said, "Take the wine cup and offer the blessing."

The other replied, "No, the host should say the blessing in his own house."

Yannai said, "Can you, at least, repeat what I shall say?"

"Yes."

"Then repeat, 'A dog has eaten Yannai's bread.' "

At this the guest leaped up and seized Yannai, and the latter cried, "But what merit have you that you should eat at my table?"

"This," replied the other, "that I never went out of my way to be churlish, nor did I ever see two men quarreling without trying to make peace between them."

Thereupon Rabbi Yannai cried: "Woe that I should have called such a one as you a dog!"

On the eve of the Sabbath, Rabbi Meir was accustomed to preach publicly for the edification of the people. Among his congregants there was a woman who was so delighted with his discourse that she remained until he had concluded. Instructed and pleased, she went toward home to enjoy the repast which was generally prepared for the honor of the day. But she was greatly disappointed on arriving home to find the lights extinguished and her husband standing at the door in very ill-humor.

"Where have you been?" he demanded. "I have been to hear our learned rabbi preach an excellent sermon," answered the woman. "Well then," said the husband, "since the rabbi has pleased you so much, I vow that you shall not enter this house until you have spit in his face, as a reward for the entertainment he has afforded you."

The woman, astonished at so unreasonable a demand, thought at first her husband was joking, but she was soon convinced that it was no jest. The man insisted on her spitting in the rabbi's face, as the sole condition of being readmitted into the house; and as she was too pious to offer such an indignity to any person, much less to so learned a man, she remained in the street.

A charitable neighbor offered her hospitality. There she remained some time, endeavoring in vain to mollify her husband, who still persisted in his first demand. The incident was known in the town, and a report of the intransigency of the husband was communicated to Rabbi Meir, who immediately sent for the woman.

When she arrived, the rabbi asked her to be seated. Pretending to have pain in his eyes, he asked her whether she knew any remedy for it. "Master," said the woman, "I am but a poor ignorant creature; how should I know how to cure your eyes?" "Well, then," rejoined the rabbi, "do as I bid. Spit seven times in my eyes—it may produce some good."

The woman, who believed there was some virtue in that operation, after some hesitation, complied. As soon as it was done, Meir thus addressed her: "My daughter, go home and tell your husband: 'It was your desire that I should spit in the rabbi's face once. I have done so; nay, I have done more, I have spit in it seven times. Now let us be reconciled.' "

Meir's disciples, who had watched their master's conduct, protested to him that he had permitted a woman to offer him such an indignity, observing that this was the way to make the people despise the law and its teachers.

"My children," said their pious instructor, "so you think that your teacher ought to be more concerned about his honor than his Creator? Even God, blessed be He, permitted His holy name to be obliterated in order to promote peace between man and wife, and shall I consider anything as an indignity that can effect so desirable an object? Learn, then, that no act is disgraceful that tends to promote the happiness and peace of mankind. It is vice and wickedness only that can degrade us."

✳ Hillel taught: "Be of the disciples of Aaron, loving peace and pursuing peace, loving your fellow creatures and drawing them near to the Torah."

✳ A lady asked what God had been doing since creation. Rabbi Josef ben Halafta replied: "He has been building ladders for some to ascend and for others to descend."

Man is endowed with the freedom of will to ascend or descend the ladder of God.

The following homily suggests that God gives man such a choice. If he chooses correctly, he may, with Divine assistance, bring about a society of justice and peace:

✳ It was taught in the name of Rabbi Eleazar: The sword and the Book were given from heaven wrapped together. The Holy One, blessed be He, said to Israel: "If you keep what is written in this Book you will be delivered from the sword, and if not, the latter will ultimately kill you."

What applies to Israel applies to all the peoples and nations of the world. The sword and the Book are given in each generation. It is not enough to choose the Book containing the will of God. Man must "keep what is written in this Book."

Our generation, too, is offered a choice: the bomb or the Bible. If we choose the bomb, we will open a Pandora's box of nuclear evil that will destroy mankind. If we choose the Book of all books, the Bible, and through religious education implement its Divine teachings, then we will build a future of holiness, justice, freedom, and peace.

Chapter VI

FAITH

$\mathbf{S}$holem Asch concludes his book Kiddush Ha-shem *with the story of the young man Sholomo, who wanders from town to town in search of his family, following the terrible massacre of the Jews in Poland in 1648. In Lublin he learned of the death of his father and mother. Bereft of family and friends, he roamed about through the fair of Lublin among the refugees. Listening to the cries and moans of his people—orphans for their parents, wives for their husbands—he yielded to despair. Could there be a future for his people? Why did a merciful God permit the destruction of so many innocent people?*

He walked in a narrow street in Lublin where the merchants' stalls were located. And he saw standing before an empty booth an old man who was calling buyers into his booth. He marvelled greatly, for the booth was

empty, and there was nothing in it to sell. He walked
into the booth and asked the old man: "What do you sell
here? Your booth is void and empty, and there is no
merchandise in it."
    And the old man answered: "I sell faith."
    And he looked intently at the old man, and the old
man appeared to him familiar as though he had seen him
before.

Sholomo had seen him before. He was Abraham at Mt.
Moriah, Moses at the Red Sea, Amos at Beth El. He was the
symbol of the faith that derives from the confrontation of God.
    While this is an intriguing story, according to Judaism
faith may not be sold. It must be acquired through study,
prayer, and meditation—and then applied.

🪶 Rabbi Simlai expounded the following:
    Six hundred and thirteen commandments were given
to Moses—365 prohibitory (thou shalt not) laws,
equaling the number of days of the solar year, and 248
mandatory (thou shalt) laws, corresponding to the
bones of man.
    David came and condensed them to eleven. As it is
written:

> Lord, who shall sojourn in Thy
>   tabernacle?
> Who shall dwell upon Thy holy
>   mountain?
> He that walketh uprightly, and worketh
>   righteousness,
> And speaketh truth in his heart;
> That hath no slander upon his tongue,
> Nor doeth evil to his fellow,
> Nor taketh up a reproach against his
>   neighbour;

In whose eyes a vile person is despised;
But he honoureth them that fear the
  Lord;
He that sweareth to his own hurt, and
  changeth not;
He that putteth not out his money on
  interest,
Nor taketh a bribe against the innocent.
He that doeth these things shall never
  be moved.

Psalm 15

Isaiah came and condensed them to six. As it is written:

He that walketh righteously, and
  speaketh uprightly;
He that despiseth the gain of
  oppressions,
That shaketh his hands from holding of
  bribes,
That stoppeth his ears from hearing of
  blood,
And shutteth his eyes from looking
  upon evil.

Isaiah 33:15

Micah came and condensed them to three. For it is written:

It hath been told thee, O man, what is
  good,
And what the Lord doth require of
  thee:
Only to do justly, and to love mercy,
  and to walk humbly with thy God.

Micah 6:8

Amos condensed them to two. As it is written:

> Thus saith the LORD unto the house of
>   Israel:
> Seek ye Me, and live.

Amos 5:4

To this Rab Nahman bar Isaac objected and said: "That would mean, 'Seek Me' in observing the entire Torah 'and live'! But it is Habakkuk who came and comprised them in one. As it is written: 'But the righteous shall live by his faith' " (Habbakuk 2:4).

🔲 A cart driver came to Rabbi Akiba and said to him: "Rabbi, teach me the whole Torah all at once." He replied: "My son, Moses our teacher stayed on the mount forty days and forty nights before he learned it, and you want me to teach you the whole of it at once! Still, my son, this is the basic principle of the Torah: What is hateful to yourself, do not to your fellow man. If you wish no one to deprive you of what is yours, you must not deprive your fellow man of what belongs to him."

The man rejoined his companions, and they journeyed until they came to a field full of seedpods. His companions each took two, but he took none. They continued their journey and came to a field full of cabbages. They each took two, but he took none. They asked him why he had not taken any, and he replied: "Thus did Rabbi Akiba teach me, 'What is hateful to yourself, do not to your fellow man.' "

🔲 According to the Midrash, before God offered the Torah to the children of Israel, He offered it to the peoples of the world. First to the Amalekites. They asked: "What is in it?" God said: "Thou shalt not kill!" The Amalekites rejected it because of the prohibition against murder. The Torah was then offered to the Ishmaelites who asked: "What is in it?" God answered: "Thou shalt not steal!" The Ishmaelites rejected it because they lived by plundering caravans in the desert. God offered the Torah to the Moabites, who asked: "What is in it?" When God replied: "Thou shalt not commit adultery!" they rejected it because of the daughters of Moab. God offered the Torah to the other peoples. When they heard the moral requirements, they rejected it. At last God offered the Torah to the children of Israel, who responded: *"Na-aseh v'nishma."* ("We will do and we will obey.") Doing must take precedence. They did not say: "We will listen [obey] and then do," but "We will *do* first, and then we will understand."

A notorious gangster, on being interrogated about religion, said: "I don't know much about religion. But I'm as religious as the next guy. I believe in the Ten Commandments!"

While we resent such a mockery of religion, it is well to consider how many well-meaning and ostensibly religious people profess their belief but fail to live by these commandments. Somebody figured it out: We have thirty-five million laws trying to enforce the Ten Commandments.

Imagine what would happen to our society if those who believe in the Ten Commandments would really live by them for twenty-four hours. What a moral revolution would ensue!

Scripture relates that when Moses descended from the mountaintop to behold the children of Israel cavorting around the golden calf in pagan revelry, in his anger, he dropped the tablets of the law, shattering them into many pieces.

☙ The rabbis ask: "Was it right for Moses to do this? Despite his anger, did he not sin in casting God's tablets of the law to the ground?"

They answered: "When Moses descended from Sinai and beheld the children of Israel violating each of the commandments, the letters on the tablets took wing and flew away. All that remained was stone—so heavy that the tablets dropped from Moses' hands to be shattered upon the earth."

This may be applied to our secular and religious institutions today. When the Spirit of God departs, all that remains is stone, wood, and iron. Without the Spirit of God, such a structure or institution becomes too burdensome to survive.

It is not enough for us to expect God to help us unless we make the effort to apply our faith and, with the inspiration of God, proceed to help ourselves.

Commenting on Exodus 14:15, "And the LORD said unto Moses: 'Wherefore criest thou unto Me? speak unto the children of Israel, that they go forward,'" the rabbis offer the following homily:

☙ In the exodus from Egypt the children of Israel were startled to hear the pursuing chariots of Pharaoh. Ahead of them was the turbulent water of the Red Sea. Hemmed in by the chariots of Pharaoh and the sea, at that moment of crisis there were four groups that offered counsel. The first group said: "We are lost. Let us plunge into the sea and die!" The second group said: "Let us return to slavery in Egypt. Perhaps the Egyptians will permit us to live." The third group said: "Let us raise our voices unto the heights of heaven in protest to God." The fourth group said: "We will not plunge into the sea to die. We will not return to slavery in Egypt. We will not limit ourselves to protests to God.

With faith in God, let us go forward into the sea and advance to the promised land." It was then that the Lord, favoring the counsel of the fourth group, said unto Moses: "Wherefore criest thou unto Me? Speak unto the children of Israel, that they go forward."

❧ A miracle was not performed at once and the Red Sea did not divide immediately. The children of Israel had to first demonstrate their faith in God by their own efforts. They advanced into the sea. The water came up to their ankles, then their knees, then their thighs. Still they proceeded into the sea. The water came up to the stomach, the chest, the neck. It was only when the water came up to the nose that the "Lord caused the sea to go back by a strong east wind all the night, and made the sea dry land, and the waters were divided."

This midrash is strikingly applicable to our own era. At a time of crisis and decision, there are generally four groups offering counsel. The first, yielding to despair, exclaims: "We are doomed. Let us commit suicide." The second, "Let us submit to totalitarianism and yield our freedom for the sake of security." The third, "Let us petition and protest, holding mass meetings and demonstrations." The fourth, "With faith in God, let us go forward."

It is significant to note that the miracle of the Red Sea was not performed until the children of Israel first demonstrated faith through action.

❧ Man must not place his sole reliance upon a mystical dependence upon prayer and study alone.

Simeon ben Yochai and his son had fled from the Roman authorities and had hid in a cave for twelve years, devoting themselves to prayer and study. When the emperor died, they emerged from the cave, and seeing a man plowing and sowing, they exclaimed: "Let us forsake life eternal and engage in life temporal." According to the legend, whatever they cast their eyes upon was immediately burned up. Thereupon, a heavenly voice cried out: "Have you emerged to destroy My world? Return to your cave."

Commenting upon this, the rabbis taught that religion must be applied to both the hope of eternal life and the practical affairs of the world. The pious must not escape into caves of mysticism or limit their faith to prayer and study alone. When we seek solutions to the problems of society, the rabbis remind us of the commandment of Deuteronomy:

This commandment which I command thee this day, it is not too hard for thee, neither is it far off. It is not in heaven, that thou shouldst say: "Who shall go up for us to heaven, and bring it unto us, and make us to hear it, that we may do it?" Neither is it beyond the sea, that thou shouldst say: "Who shall go over the sea for us, and bring it unto us, and make us to hear it, that we may do it?" But the word is very nigh unto thee, in thy mouth, and in they heart, *that thou mayest do it* (Deuteronomy 30:11–14).

God has given man the freedom of will to apply his faith by making a moral choice. "See, I have set before thee this day life and good, and death and evil, in that I command thee this day to love the LORD thy God, to walk in His ways, and to keep His commandments and His statutes and His ordinances" (Deuteronomy 30:15–16).

A rabbi and a soapmaker went for a walk together. The soapmaker said: "What good is religion? Look at the trouble and the misery in the world after thousands of years of teaching about goodness, truth, and peace—after all the prayers and sermons and teachings. If religion is good and true, why should this be?"

The rabbi said nothing. They continued walking until he noticed a child playing in the gutter. The child was filthy with mud and grime. Then the rabbi said: "Look at that child. You say that soap makes people clean, but see the dirt on that youngster? Of what good is soap? With all the soap in the world, that child is still filthy. I wonder just how effective soap is after all?"

The soapmaker protested and said: "But, Rabbi, soap can't do any good unless it's used!"

"Exactly," replied the rabbi. "So it is with Judaism or any religion. It isn't effective unless it is applied and used."

Rabbi Levi Yitzhak once summoned the townspeople to meet in the town square to hear an important announcement. The merchant resented having to leave his business. The housewife protested against leaving her chores. However, obedient to their rabbi, the townspeople gathered together to hear the announcement their teacher was to make.

When all were present, Rabbi Levi Yitzhak said: "I wish to announce that there is a God in the world."

That was all he said, but the people understood. They had been acting as if God did not exist. While they observed ritual and recited the correct order of prayers, their actions did not comply with the commandments of God. The rabbi's announcement to the people was a cogent reminder that to act immorally or unethically is to suggest that there is no God.

The rabbinic concept of faith is predicated on the belief in a moral and ethical God. Without God there can be no religious authority for faith, morality, or ethical values.

When Rabbi Samuel visited Rome, he found a bracelet. The empress announced that she had lost a precious bracelet and offered a huge reward if it was returned in thirty days. Should the finder fail to return it in this time, he would forfeit his head.

Rabbi Samuel waited until the thirty days had passed before he returned the bracelet. He then admitted to the empress that he had known of her promise and her threat.

In reply to the perplexed look on her face, the rabbi told her: "You must know that ethical conduct is inspired neither by hope of reward nor fear of punishment. It stems solely from the love of God and the desire to do His commandments."

Faith in God requires not only the belief in God, but a commitment to morality. This faith must be exemplified by a life of ma-asim Tovim *(good deeds). Man must demonstrate his obedience to God's way by kindness and service to God's children.*

Rabbi Israel of Rizhyn told of a poor villager who came to town to earn money for the Passover. As he returned to the village after nightfall, his horse and wagon fell into a swampy pit. A rich man passing by heard his cries and rescued the villager. He tied the latter's wagon to his carriage and conducted the poor man to his hut. On beholding the abject poverty of the villager and his family, the wealthy man gave him several hundred thalers.

When the rich man died and was brought before the heavenly tribunal, it appeared that his demerits would disqualify him from paradise. Suddenly an angel of mercy appeared and asked that the heavenly scales be used to determine whether his good deeds outweighed his sins. When consent was given, the angel placed on the scale of good deeds the poor villager and his family whom the rich man had delivered from misery. But this was not sufficient. The horse and wagon were added, but to no avail. Then the angel placed on the scale the mud and mire out of which the rich man had rescued the villager, and lo, the scale of good deeds dipped with its weight, and the rich man was allowed to enter heaven.

⚘ At dusk on a Sabbath eve Abba Tahnah the pious was entering his city, with his bundle slung over his shoulder, when he encountered a man afflicted with boils lying at the crossroads. The latter said to him, "Rabbi, do me an act of charity and carry me into the city." He remarked, "If I abandon my bundle, from where shall I and my household support themselves? But if I abandon this afflicted man, I will forfeit my life!"

What did he do? He allowed the good inclination to master the evil inclination and carried the afflicted man into the city. He then returned for his bundle and entered at sunset. Everybody was astonished and exclaimed, "Is this Abba Tahnah the pious?" He too felt uneasy in his heart and said, "Alas, I have desecrated the Sabbath!"

At that time the Holy One, blessed be He, caused the sun to shine, as it is written, "But unto you that fear My name shall the sun of righteousness arise" (Malachi 3:20). Abba Tahnah was thus saved from violating the Sabbath and traveling at night.

A ritual observance is primarily for the purpose of symbolizing an ethical ideal. Sometimes it becomes necessary to omit a required ritual or observance in order to help one's fellow man. To understand this story of Abba Tahnah it must be remembered that to travel after sundown on Friday evening is regarded as a violation of the Sabbath, which is to be observed as a day of rest. By his act of kindness, Abba Tahnah inadvertently had to enter the town at sunset. Despite the Jewish insistence upon the careful and reverent observance of the Sabbath ritual and regulations, the rabbis regarded an act of kindness as sufficiently important to justify Abba Tahnah before man and God. This was his ethical response motivated by his faith.

※ Rabbi Judah the Prince taught: "A single commandment, properly performed in purity of heart, may cause one to inherit eternal life. A single deed may be of such great merit as to atone for a lifetime of sins and raise a man to the level of the saint."

※ The Hasidic rabbi Yitzhak Meir taught his disciples the futility of torturing themselves with remorse over past sins, saying: "He who reflects on the evil he has done is thinking evil, and what one thinks, therein is one caught. Stir filth however you will, and it is still filth. In the time that I am brooding, I could be stringing pearls for the sake of heaven. Thus it is written: 'Depart from evil, and do good.' Turn wholly from evil; do not brood over it, but do good."

RELIGIOUS EDUCATION

The rabbis found it difficult to conceive of faith without religious education. "An ignorant man cannot be pious" was the dictum of the sages. This is not meant to create an aristocracy of the learned, nor is this to be interpreted as contempt for the uneducated, but one who is religiously ignorant cannot be pious.

⚜ A rabbi taught: "If I were to set out to give learned and subtle interpretations of the Scriptures, I could say a great many things. But a fool says what he knows, while a sage knows what he says."

⚜ A young rabbi complained to the rabbi of Rizhyn: "During the hours when I devote myself to my studies I feel life and light, but the moment I stop studying, the feeling is gone. What shall I do?"

The rabbi of Rizhyn replied: "That is just as when a man makes his way through the forest on a dark night, and for a time another joins him, lantern in hand; but when they part at the crossroads, the first must grope on alone. If a man carries his own light with him, he need never to be afraid of darkness."

⚜ As evidence of a man without secular knowledge but whose study of the Torah has sustained him with faith, there is the story of one who complained to a Hasidic rabbi that God had cursed him with anguish, sorrow, and misfortune. He asked the rabbi to give him advice so that he would be able to bear his fate.

The rabbi said: "I cannot help you. Go rather to Isaac the water carrier, who has suffered every sorrow and misfortune that can happen to man. Let him help you."

The man sought out Isaac the water carrier and explained why the rabbi had sent him. After listening, Isaac looked up in amazement and said: "I cannot understand why the holy rabbi has sent you to see me. I have never suffered a misfortune in my life."

Isaac's faith was such that everything in life testified to the wisdom and goodness of God.

The Torah, which records the revelation of God, is available and accessible to all. Anyone who thirsts for the knowledge of

God may come and drink of the living waters of the Torah. Let no one say that he has neither the time nor the inclination for learning.

🔯 A rabbi narrates: "I was once accosted by a man who said to me: 'Rabbi, I am entirely unlearned; I do not even know the Pentateuch.'

"I asked him why he did not study, and he replied: 'Because my Father in heaven did not give me understanding and discernment.'

"I said: 'What is thy occupation?'

" 'I am a fisherman,' he answered.

" 'And who taught thee to weave nets and to spread them properly for the catch?'

"The fisherman replied: 'Understanding and discernment were given me from heaven for this purpose.'

"I said: 'If God gave thee understanding wherewith to catch fish, did He not give thee sufficient intelligence to learn His Torah, concerning which He has written: "It is not too hard for thee, neither is it far off. . . . But the Word is very nigh unto thee" ' (Deuteronomy 30:11–14).

"The fisherman began to weep and to sigh. I said to him: 'Be not sad of heart. Other persons have argued like thee, but their occupations betrayed them and brought their arguments to naught. It is never too late to learn.' "

🔯 Rabbi Ammi quoted, "Wisdom is as unattainable to a fool as corals" (Proverbs 24:7). Rabbi Johanan said: "This may be compared to a loaf hanging high up in a house. A fool says: 'Who can bring this down?' A sensible person says: 'Has not some person hung it up?' He then fetches two rods, ties them one to another, and brings it down. So, too, the fool says: 'Who can learn the whole of the Torah that is in the heart of a scholar?' whereas the sensible person says: 'Has not he [the scholar] learned it from another? I shall learn two *halachoth* [laws] today, and two tomorrow, until I have learned the whole Torah.' "

No matter what book Rabbi Mikhal was reading, whether a book of the open or the hidden teachings, everything he read seemed to him to point to the service of God. When one of his disciples asked him how this was possible, he replied: "Could there be anything in the teachings which does not point out to us how to serve God?"

The Holy One, blessed be He, said to Israel: "My children, I have created the evil impulse, and I have created the Torah as an antidote to it; if you occupy yourselves with the Torah, you will not be delivered into its power."

The study of the Torah is the obligation of every Jew. Since Judaism is a religious faith, and not a race or a nationality, a Jew without religion is like a body without a soul.

Despite oppression, hatred, and persecution, every Jew must cleave loyally to his faith.

The authorities in Rome had issued a decree forbidding the Jews to study the Torah. Thereupon, Rabbi Akiba arose and, at the risk of his life, sent about from town to town establishing academies. He himself held forth in learned discourse to great throngs.

One day Rabbi Akiba met Rabbi Pappus ben Yehuda, the sage and patriot. "Aren't you afraid of the authorities?" asked Pappus.

"You speak like a fool, Pappus, even though many people think you're wise!" exclaimed Rabbi Akiba. And the latter told the following parable:

A fox one day was walking along the shore of a lake. He noticed that the little fish were scurrying to and fro in the water. As he looked at them he had a great desire to eat them.

"Foolish little fish. . . . Why do you scurry about like that?" he asked them.

"We are fleeing from the nets of the fisherman," the fish replied.

"In that case," replied the sly fox, "why don't you come ashore, and we will live like brothers, just as your parents did with mine."

The little fish replied, "O you foxy one. You talk like a fool even though many think you clever. What silly advice are you giving us? If we are in constant fear of our lives in the place where we are and live, how do you suppose it will be on dry land where we cannot live? Surely death awaits us there."

Then Rabbi Akiba continued: "It is with us Jews the same as it was with the little fishes. We are afraid of the enemy even when we study the Torah, which is our support and life. Can you imagine what fear would fall upon us were we to abandon this study, since it is said of the Torah, 'It is thy life, and the length of thy days'?" (Deuteronomy 30:20).

Rabbi Huna, in the name of Rabbi Benjamin ben Levi, said: "The matter may be compared to the case of a king who said to his son, 'Go out and do business.' Said the son to him: 'Father, I am afraid of robbers on the road and of pirates on the sea.' What did his father do? He took a staff, hollowed it out, and placed an amulet inside it. He gave it to his son and said to him:

'Let this staff be in your hand and you need not be afraid of any creature.' So also did the Holy One, blessed be He, say to Moses: 'Tell Israel: "My children! Occupy yourselves with the Torah and you need not be afraid of any nation." ' "

৯ The soul and the Torah are compared to a lamp: the soul, as it is written, "The spirit of man is the lamp of the LORD" (Proverbs 20:27); and the law, as it is written, "For the commandment is a lamp, and the teaching is light" (Proverbs 6:23). God said to man: "My light, My Torah, is in your hand, and your light, your soul, is in My hand. If you will guard My light, I will guard your light, but if you will extinguish My light, I will extinguish your light."

The Torah is not the legacy of the wise alone. It does not belong only to the scholars, the priests, or the rich. It is the inheritance of the entire congregation of Israel.

In order to assure devotion to the Torah, which means living by its precepts, it is incumbent upon the parents and the community to begin the instruction of children at an early age.

The following homily demonstrates the significance of children as the surety for the future:

৯ Although the people had now clearly expressed their desire to accept the Torah, still God hesitated to give it to them, saying: "Shall I without further ado give you the Torah? Nay, bring Me bondsmen, that you will observe it, and I will give you the Torah." Israel: "O Lord of the world! Our fathers are bondsmen for us." God said: "Your fathers are My debtors, and therefore not good bondsmen. Abraham said, 'Whereby shall I know it?' and thus proved himself lacking in faith. Isaac

loved Esau, whom I hated, and Jacob did not immediately upon his return from Paddan-aram keep his vow
that he made upon his way there. Bring Me good
bondsmen and I will give you the Torah." Israel: "Our
prophets shall be our bondsmen." God said: "I have
claims against them, for 'like foxes in the deserts
became your prophets.' Bring Me good bondsmen and
I will give you the Torah." Israel: "We will give Thee
our children as bondsmen." God said: "These are good
bondsmen. With the assurance that your children will
obey my commandments, I will give you the Torah."

Rabbi Judah asked Rabbi Dosa and Rabbi Ammi to
go forth and inspect the cities in the land of Israel. They
came to a city and said to the people, "Have the keepers
of the city brought before us."

The people brought the overseers. Then they said to
them: "Are these the keepers of the city?"

The people then brought forth the generals, the rich
men, and the strongest of the city, but the rabbis asked:
"Are these the keepers of the city?"

Then the people asked the rabbis: "Who then are the
keepers of the city?"

The rabbis answered: "The teachers of the scriptures
and the tradition, who keep watch by day and by night,
in accordance with these words: 'This book of the law
shall not depart out of thy mouth, but thou shalt
meditate therein day and night.'"

According to the Midrash, it was not the virtue of the
Jews that saved them from destruction at the hands of
the tyrant Haman. What then saved the Jews of Persia?

Having made the gallows, Haman went to Mordecai,
whom he found in the house of study. Before Mordecai
sat the school children, studying the Torah and weeping. Haman counted them and found there 22,000

children. He put them in chains, saying, "Tomorrow I will kill these children first, and then I will hang Mordecai."

Their mothers brought them bread and water and said to them: "Children, eat and drink before you die tomorrow." Straightaway the children swore by the life of Mordecai their teacher, saying, "We will neither eat nor drink, but will die while still fasting."

The sound of their cry ascended to heaven and the Holy One, blessed be He, heard the sound of their weeping at about the second hour of the night. At that moment His compassion was stirred, and He arose from the throne of judgment and sat on the throne of mercy and said: "What is this loud noise that I hear as the bleating of kids and lambs?"

Moses our teacher thereupon stood before the Holy One, blessed be He, and said: "Sovereign of the universe, they are neither kids nor lambs, but the little ones of Thy people who have been keeping a fast now for three days and for three nights, and tomorrow the enemy means to slaughter them."

At that moment the Holy One, blessed be He, took the letters containing their doom, which were signed with a seal of clay, and tore them and brought fright upon Ahasuerus in that night, as it says, "On that night could not the king sleep; and he commanded to bring the book of records" (Esther 6:1).[1]

A disciple asked the Baal Shem, "Why is it that one who clings to God and knows he is close to Him sometimes experiences a sense of interruption and remoteness?"

---

[1] The book of records revealed that Mordecai had saved the king's life. Thus the Jews of Persia escaped destruction – through the cries of the children.

The Baal Shem explained: "When a father starts to teach his child to walk, he stands in front of him and holds out his hands on either side of the child so that he cannot fall, and the boy goes toward his father. But the moment the child is close, his father withdraws a little and holds his hands farther apart. As the father does this again and again, the child learns to walk."

RELIGIOUS TEACHERS AND LEADERS

The position of teacher was a coveted one in the Jewish tradition. The teacher was the leader and was charged not only with the duty of imparting religious knowledge, but of leading the congregation and the community in the paths of God.

Patience is a requisite for any religious teacher. The Midrash relates a homily on the verse "And the patient in spirit is better than the proud in spirit":

A Persian came to Rab and said to him, "Teach me the Torah." Rab consented and, pointing to the first letter of the alphabet, told him, "Say *aleph*." The man remarked, "Who says that this is *aleph*? There may be others who say that it is not!" Rab commanded, "Say *beth*," to which he remarked, "Who says that this is *beth*?" Rab rebuked him and drove him out in anger.

The Persian went to Samuel and said to him, "Teach me the Torah." He told him, "Say *aleph*." The man remarked, "Who says that this is *aleph*?" The teacher took hold of his ear, and the man exclaimed, "My ear! My ear!" Samuel asked him, "Who said that this is your ear?" He answered, "Everybody knows that this is my ear," and the teacher retorted, "In the same way everybody knows that this is *aleph* and that this is *beth*."

Immediately the Persian was silenced and accepted the instruction.

🐾 Commenting on the verse "And she went to inquire of the LORD" (Genesis 25:22), the rabbis asked: "Were there then synagogues and houses of study in those days [of Rebekah]? Surely she went only to the college of Shem and Eber? Hence this teaches you that to visit a sage is like visiting the Divine Presence."

🐾 Another rabbi taught that those who minister to the congregation and serve as teachers must ever be humble. They must never assume that the respect and homage that is expressed for religion is meant as reverence for those who are the leaders and teachers. He expounded this homily: "When the ark of the covenant was being transported on a cart pulled by cows, the laborers along the wayside bowed in reverence before the Holy Ark. Upon seeing this, the cows exclaimed: 'See how men bow to us! Behold the reverence that is shown to us. Truly, we are favored of God.' However, when the ark was taken into the Holy of Holies, the cows were led forth to be slaughtered."

🐾 Our Teacher was passing Simonia, when its inhabitants came out to meet him and requested him, saying: "Rabbi, give us a man to teach us Scripture and Mishnah and be our judge." He gave them Levi, the son of Sisi. They erected a great platform and set him upon it, but he forgot some of his learning. They asked him three questions, but he could not answer them. When he saw in what a sorry plight he was, he arose early in the morning and repaired to our teacher.

"What did the inhabitants of Simonia do to you?" the rabbi inquired. "Do not remind me of my troubles,"

Levi rejoined: "They asked me three questions, and I could not answer them. But I know the answers now." "Then why did you not answer them as you have answered me?" his teacher demanded. "They erected a great platform for me and set me upon it," Levi answered, "and that made me conceited and so I forgot my learning." Thereupon the rabbi applied to him this verse: "If thou hast done foolishly in lifting up thyself."

The tenth chapter of Leviticus tells of the death of Nadab and Abihu, the sons of Aaron, who offered "strange fire" before the Lord. "And there came forth fire from before the LORD, and devoured them, and they died before the LORD."

What were the sins of Nadab and Abihu? According to the rabbis, only their souls were consumed; their bodies remained untouched. This means that they died religiously.

The explanation is that Nadab and Abihu dared to enter the sanctuary under the influence of drink. We are then reminded of the following midrash:

When Noah, after the Deluge, planted the vine, Satan approached him and said: "What are you planting?" "The vine," answered Noah. "Let me help you," said Satan. "I will bring you excellent manure." Noah accepted the offer. Then Satan went and got himself a ewe, a lion, a pig, and an ape; he slaughtered these, one after another, and poured their blood into the ground where the vine was planted. "So much for the man," said Satan to himself, and he was filled with joy. "From now on he will drink in with the wine all the vices of these beasts whose blood is mingled with the vine: if he will drink a little, he will be soft like the sheep; if he drink much, he will be haughty and quarrelsome like the lion; if he drink still more, he will become like the pig, and like the pig will roll in his filth;

and if he drink more still, he will be laughable, like the ape, and like the ape will babble madness."

Another explanation for the religious death of Nadab and Abihu is that they were jealous of Moses and Aaron, and asked themselves, "When will these old men die? How long must we wait to lead the congregation?" Unfilial jealousy and impious ambition prompted them to approach the altar in a spirit of envy and hatred.

Following the religious death of Nadab and Abihu, Moses said to Aaron, "This is what God meant when He said, 'Through them that are nigh unto Me I will be sanctified, and before all the people I will be glorified'" (Leviticus 10:3). The rabbis explained: "Judaism teaches that the greater a man's knowledge or position, the stricter the standard by which he is judged, and the greater the consequent guilt if there are deviations from the laws of morality, since the Talmud admonishes: 'With the righteous, God is exacting, even to a hair's breadth.'"

A man came to the rabbi of Kotsk and asked how he could encourage his sons to study the Torah. The rabbi answered: "If you really want them to study, then you yourself must spend time over the Torah, and they will do likewise. Otherwise, they will not devote themselves to the Torah but will order their sons to do it, and thus it will continue. For it is written: 'Only take heed to thyself . . . lest thou forgot the things which thine eyes saw . . .; but make them known unto thy children and thy children's children.' If you yourself forget the Torah, your sons will also forget it, though urging their sons to know it, and they too will forget the Torah and tell their sons that they should know it, and no one will ever know the Torah."

How relevant is this admonition to parents! They must provide the religious example for their children because it is through the ethical behavior of parents, leaders, and teachers that God may be sanctified and glorified.

Rabbi Leib used to say about those who expounded the Torah: "What does it mean? A man should see to it that all his actions *are* a Torah and that he himself becomes so entirely a Torah that one can learn from his habits and motions and his motionless clinging to God."

His disciples used to say: "Watching Rabbi Leib tie his shoelaces is a lesson in Torah. Whatever he does, his actions are one with Torah."

Apparently the preachers of long ago encountered the same difficulty that confronts our contemporaries, and that is to arouse the congregation from lassitude and inertia.

Rabbi Judah was once expounding the Scripture, and the congregation became drowsy. In order to rouse them he said: "One woman in Egypt brought forth six hundred thousand at a birth." There was a certain disciple there named Rabbi Ishmael, son of Rabbi Jose, who said to him: "Who can that have been?" He replied: "This was Jochebed who bore Moses, who was counted as equal to six hundred thousand of Israel"; for so it says, "Then sang Moses and the children of Israel" (Exodus 15:1); "Thus did the children of Israel; according to all that the LORD commanded Moses, so did they" (Numbers 1:54); "And there hath not arisen a prophet since in Israel like unto Moses" (Deuteronomy 34:10).

At the time of the Roman siege of Jerusalem, Rabbi Jochanan ben Zakkai said, "I have come to the conclusion that I must get out of here." He sent a message to Ben Battiah, "Get me out of here." He replied, "We have made an agreement among ourselves that nobody shall leave the city except the dead." He said, "Carry me out in the guise of a corpse." Rabbi Eliezer carried him by the head, Rabbi Joshua by the feet, and Ben Battiah walked in front. When they reached the city gates, the guards wanted to stab the supposed corpse to make certain of death. Ben Battiah said to them, "Do you wish people to say that when our teacher died his body was stabbed?" On his speaking to them in this manner, they allowed him to pass. After going through the gates, they carried him to a cemetery and left him there and returned to the city.

Rabbi Jochanan ben Zakkai came out and went among the soldiers of Vespasian. He said to them, "Where is the king?" They went and told Vespasian, "A Jew is asking for you." He said to them, "Let him come." On his arrival the rabbi exclaimed, *"Vive domine Imperator!"* Vespasian remarked, "You give me a royal greeting but I am not king; and should the king hear of it he will put me to death." The rabbi said to him, "If you are not the king, you will be eventually, because the Temple will be destroyed only by a king's hand"; as it is said, "And Lebanon shall fall by a mighty one" (Isaiah 10:34).

Three days later Vespasian went to take a bath at Gophna. After he had bathed and put on one of his shoes, a message arrived and it was announced to him that Nero had died and the Romans had proclaimed him king.

Ultimately Rabbi Jochanan ben Zakkai was told by Vespasian that any request he would make would be granted. The rabbi asked for permission to open a school at Jabneh. This wish was granted, and in time

Jabneh became a great academy of learning; but even more, it saved Judaism from destruction. With the Temple destroyed and the land desolate, the academy at Jabneh kept alive the study and the teaching of Judaism. It became a center of religious hope that made for the perpetuation of the Jewish faith.

Moses is regarded as the greatest of the prophets. Easily provoked to Divine anger, yet he was the meekest of men. He was summoned to leadership because of the attribute of infinite tenderness that characterized his ministry.

🦌 Moses, our teacher, was tested by God through sheep. When Moses was tending the flock of Jethro in the wilderness, a little kid escaped him. He ran after it until it reached a shady place. When it reached the shady place, there appeared to view a pool of water, and the kid stopped to drink. When Moses approached it, he said: "I did not know that you ran away because of thirst; you must be weary." So he placed the kid on his shoulder and walked away. Thereupon God said: "Because thou hast mercy in leading the flock of a mortal, thou wilt assuredly tend My flock Israel."

The religious teacher, according to the rabbis, must endeavor to emulate the tenderness of Moses and show compassion not only for the children of God, but for all creatures.

🦌 The Baal Shem said to a zaddik who used to preach admonishing sermons: "What do you know about admonishing! You yourself have remained unacquainted with sin all the days of your life, and you have had nothing to do with the people around you—how should you know what sinning is!"

The Hebrew text describes Moses descending from the mountaintop with light emanating from him because of his encounter with God. The famous picture of Moses by Michelangelo depicts him with horns. This resulted from an error on the part of the famous artist, who translated the word keren *as "horn" rather than "ray of light."*

🕮 "Moses knew not that the skin of his face sent forth beams" (Exodus 34:29). Rabbi Judah ben Nahman said: "A little ink was left on the pen with which Moses wrote the Decalogue, and when he passed his pen through the hair of his head [to dry the pen], the beams of splendor appeared; hence does it say: 'Moses knew not that the skin of his face sent forth beams.' "

Just as some of the Divine luster accrued to Moses because of his intimate relationship to God, so the teacher may bring Divine influence to bear upon his students and bring them into the light of God.

The manner in which Moses relinquished leadership to his successor indicates the essential humility of the great.

🕮 As the hour approached when Joshua was accustomed to arise, Moses entered his room and extended his hand to him. When Joshua saw that Moses served him, he was ashamed to have it so, and taking the garments from Moses' hand, he dressed himself, and fell trembling at Moses' feet.

"O my master," said Joshua, "be not the cause wherefore I should die, owing to the sovereignty God has imposed upon me." But Moses replied: "Fear not, my son, thou sinnest not if thou art served by me. It was I that taught thee, 'Love thy neighbor as thyself,' and also, 'Let thy pupil's honor be as dear to thee as thine own.' "

Then Moses seated Joshua upon the golden chair and served him in every needful way. Thereafter he laid upon Joshua, who still resisted, his rays of majesty, which had been given him by the scribe of the angels at the close of his instruction in the Torah.

When Joshua was ready to go out, it was reported to him and to Moses that all Israel awaited them. Moses thereupon conducted Joshua from the tent and insisted upon giving precedence to him as they stepped forth. When Israel saw Joshua precede Moses, they all trembled, arose, and made room for them to advance to the place of honor, where stood the golden throne. Moses seated Joshua upon it, though the latter protested. All Israel burst into tears when they saw Joshua upon the golden throne, and he said amid tears: "Why all this honor to me?"

Moses now said to himself: "If God has determined that I may not enter the land of Israel, for no other reason than because the time has come for my disciple Joshua to assume leadership, then were it better for me to remain alive, and not die, but serve the new leader."

What now did Moses do? From the first day of Shebat to the sixth of Adar,[2] the day before his death, he went and served Joshua from morning until evening, as a disciple his master. These thirty-six days during which Moses served his former disciple corresponded to the equal number of years during which he had been served by Joshua.

One of the most beautiful of the midrashim extolling religious leadership is the homily on the verse from Genesis, "Thus shall be thy seed." What is meant by "Thus shall be thy seed"?

---

[2]Hebrew months.

Rabbi Levi, in the name of Rabbi Johanan, told of a man who set out on a journey and traveled a day, two days, three days, up to ten days, without finding either town or wayside inn, or tree, or water, or any living creature. After having traveled ten days, when he was about to relinquish all hope, he espied a tree in the distance and thought, "There may be water beneath it." When he approached quite close, he found that it indeed stood by a fountain. Seeing how beautiful the tree was, and how excellent the fruit, and how beautiful the boughs, he sat down and cooled himself in its shade. Then he partook of the fruit, drank at the fountain, and felt pleased and refreshed.

When he rose up to go he said, apostrophizing the tree: "What blessing can I bestow upon thee or what parting word can I offer thee? That thy wood shall be fine? It is fine. That thy shade shall be pleasant? It is pleasant already. That thy boughs shall be fair? They are fair. That thy fruits shall be luscious? Luscious they are. That a fountain shall flow beneath thy roots? A fountain already flows beneath thy roots. That thou shouldst stand in a desirable spot? Why, thou dost stand in a desirable spot. What blessing, then, can I bestow upon thee? Only that all the saplings that shall spring from thee may be like unto thee. 'Thus shall be thy seed.'"

How can we give expression to our gratitude to the leaders and teachers who instruct us in the ways of God? That they may be blessed with wisdom, eloquence, virtue, honor? Behold, they have already been blessed with these qualities. What blessing then may we invoke upon them? Only that all who come under their influence may be like unto them. "Thus shall be thy spiritual descendants."

The concept of faith, as reflected in the Talmud, the

Midrash, and Hasidic literature, is derived from the belief in the moral God. Even when reason may be inclined to doubt the mercy and justice of God, faith insists that although we do not understand, there is a Divine wisdom that supersedes our inclinations and conclusions.

An inscription in a cellar of Cologne where Jews took refuge in flight from the Nazi terror bears witness to this. The inscription reads as follows: "I believe in the sun, even when it is not shining. I believe in love, even when feeling it not. I believe in God, even when He is silent."

A Jew is to believe in God, even when it seems that God is silent. His belief must motivate him to faith in God despite the absence of godliness in the society in which he lives.

What was understood by faith may be gathered from the statement of the rabbis: "Whoever has a morsel of bread in his basket and says, 'What shall I eat tomorrow?' belongs only to those who are small of faith."

Belief and moral action are indivisible. It is not enough to believe without manifesting belief through our deeds. The strength of a living faith sustains us through the valley of the shadow of death, through darkness, sorrow, illness, and failure. These experiences of life are of the moment. God is from everlasting to everlasting. It is through religious faith that man identifies himself with eternity.

Chapter VII

ETERNAL LIFE

Whenen Rabbi Bunam lay dying, his wife burst into tears. He said: "What are you crying for? My whole life was only that I might learn how to die."

Judaism does not permit a morbid preoccupation with death. The Jewish identity is with life. Death is recognized as an inevitable concomitant of God's Divine plan for His creatures. Therefore, death is anticipated without horror, but with abiding faith in the goodness, the love, and the mercy of God.

Commenting on the verse from Psalms, "I shall not die, but live," Rabbi Yitzhak said: "In order really to live, a man must give himself to death. But when he has done so he discovers that he is not to die—but to live."

The dictum of the Midrash, "The righteous are called living even in their death," exemplifies the conviction that those who love God go from life to life everlasting.

THE SANCTIFICATION OF GOD

Paradoxically, the prayer that Jews utter to memorialize the dead does not include one word of mourning or sorrow. Called the "Kaddish" (holiness), the prayer is a sanctification of God. It begins:

Extolled and hallowed be the name of God throughout the world which He has created according to His will. May He speedily establish His Kingdom of righteousness on earth. Amen.

Praised and glorified be the name of the Holy One, though He be above all the praises which we can utter.

Our guide is He in life and our redeemer through all eternity.

The Kaddish prayer concludes with the following supplication:

May He who maketh peace on High, may He bring peace upon us, upon Israel and all mankind. Amen.

The Kaddish is recited standing, to symbolize our reverence for God even at a time of sorrow. Moreover it is to signify that we refuse to be crushed by grief, but that we stand in dignity despite the sorrow of our hearts.

There are scholars who note a similarity between the

Kaddish and the Lord's Prayer. They assert that Jesus derived His prayer from the Kaddish and other prayers of rabbinic Judaism.

There is no pain more devastating, more intense, more difficult to accept, than the pain of grief, the excruciating torture of bereavement. With all the wonder drugs, there are no sulfas for sorrow and no antibiotics for the pain of grief. With all the advances made in modern surgery, who can mend and put together the shattered fragments of a broken heart?

The sacrifice of God, according to the psalmist, is a broken heart. To live is to experience pain, sorrow, and bereavement. How frequently is the question of the psalmist enunciated on our lips as we ask: "From whence shall come my help?" The answer of faith is the same in every generation: "My help cometh from the Lord God who made heaven and earth." At a time of grief we lift our eyes unto the heavens in quest of solace, comfort, and peace.

No appeal to God, no cry of distress, goes unanswered.

"God hears a cry of sorrow even when it is unuttered," said Rabbi Mendel. Commenting on the verse "And God heard the voice of the lad," he explained it in this way: "Nothing in the preceding verses indicates that Ishmael cried out. No, it was a soundless cry, but God heard it."

While we acknowledge the inevitability of death, we seem so shocked and surprised when death occurs to those we love. The rabbis taught that death is not a punishment visited by God, but rather a part of God's Divine plan. Man is not alone when he experiences grief. The summons to sanctify God in sorrow is universal.

A great famine spread in Israel when it was besieged by Ben-hadad, the king of Aram. As the king of Israel was passing by, "there cried a woman unto him, saying, 'Help, my lord, O king.' And he said: 'If the LORD do not help thee, whence shall I help thee?' " Then the woman told the king of her great sorrow—the loss of her son. And it came to pass that when the king heard the words of the woman, he tore his garments in grief. The people looked, and behold, they saw that beneath his outer garments, he had sackcloth within upon his flesh. Even the king of Israel had his secret sorrow.

How can we know of all those who are carrying on bravely, suffering under the weight of burdens almost too great for their endurance, and while we complain to them and even envy them, we may never see the sackcloth within. A meaningful religious faith urges us to be kind and considerate to everyone, for each person carries some secret sorrow in his heart.

There are many compelling stories that are coming to us from the state of Israel, but the following indicates how it is possible to sanctify God in sorrow by reaching out beyond our grief to help others:

There was a middle-aged couple whose only child had been killed in a concentration camp in Europe. The mother and father had found a haven in Israel, but they continued to grieve for their child. Few people knew of the sackcloth within. Through prayer they went to God and cast their burden upon the Lord—and through prayer they realized that it wasn't enough to mourn for their child; they realized that just as they were child-less, so there were children who were fatherless and motherless. Accordingly, they went to an adoption center and made application for a child. There they saw one child among the many assembled, a lovely little girl, who captured their hearts. They asked her if she would not like to live with them. The child answered that she would be willing, but that if they adopted her, they would have to adopt her little brother, too. She had promised her mother before she died that she would never be separated from her brother and that she would always look after him and care for him. The childless couple asked to see the little boy, and after a hurried consultation, they decided to adopt both children.

They took the children home with them, after buying them some new clothes. That evening, after the exciting experiences of the day, they put the children to bed. It was only a moment after they left the children that they heard the youngsters crying hysterically and uttering terrifying screams. They rushed into the room and found that the girl had taken a picture of the woman's sister off the wall and was clutching it to her chest. The children told through their tears that it was a picture of their mother.

Thus this kindly couple found that they had adopted their own niece and nephew—the children of a sister who had remained in Poland—and had given a home to children of their own blood! In the days and months that followed this reunion, the couple discovered that in devoting themselves to these orphan children, in giving of themselves to those little ones who were carrying such a burden of sorrow, they had lost the sackcloth within. It had been supplanted by a new joy, a new strength, and a new sustaining love.

There is no miraculous cure for heartache. With all the wonder drugs, there is no instant and wondrous cure for sorrow. We cannot by force of will reach in and tear the sackcloth from our souls. But we can achieve healing through faith. We can share our troubles with our Heavenly Father.

🦋 Rabbi Joseph Hertz, former chief rabbi of England, in the spirit of the Talmud, told of a traveler who was crossing mountain heights of untrodden snow alone. He struggled bravely against the sense of sleep which weighed down his eyelids, for he knew that if he fell asleep, death would be inevitable. Just then his foot struck against a heap lying across his path. Stooping down, he found it to be a human body half buried in the snow. The next moment he held the body in his arms and was rubbing the frozen man's limbs. The effort to restore another unto life brought back to himself warmth and energy, and was the means of saving both.

In Whittier's words,

> Heaven's gate is shut to him who
>   comes alone.
> Save thou a soul, and it shall save thine
>   own.

With the help of God and with unselfish service to others, we too can convert the sackcloth within into a garment of faith, of hope, of courage, and of salvation.

IS DEATH EVIL?

Is death evil? or does death serve as a messenger of God, who comes to us as a friend? ask the rabbis. Does man ever acquire enough possessions to satisfy his ambitions before he is summoned from this earth? How can man make life mean-

ingful and prepare religiously for the day of death? How can our religious faith sustain us in bereavement? What can man learn from death? What is meant by life beyond the grave? These are questions that are asked by the rabbis. They attempted to provide religious answers through stories and homilies. To them, the seventh chapter of Ecclesiastes was not a macabre jest, but was filled with profound wisdom for the living. Thus they commented on Ecclesiastes 7:1–4:

> A good name is better than precious
> oil;
> And the day of death than the day of
> one's birth.
> It is better to go to the house of
> mourning,
> Than to go to the house of feasting;
> For that is the end of all men,
> And the living will lay it to his heart,
> Vexation is better than laughter;
> For by the sadness of the countenance
> the heart may be gladdened.
> The heart of the wise is in the house of
> mourning;
> But the heart of fools is in the house of
> mirth.

Commenting on "the day of death [is better] than the day of one's birth," they relate the story of two ships:

🏺 Two ships were once seen near land. One of them was leaving the harbor, and the other was coming into it. Everyone was cheering the outgoing ship, giving it a hearty send-off. But the incoming ship was scarcely noticed.

A wise man standing nearby exclaimed: "Rejoice not over the ship that is setting out to sea, for you know not

what destiny awaits it, what storms it may encounter,
what dangers lurk before it. Rejoice rather over the ship
that has reached port safely and brought back all its
passengers in peace."

It is the way of the world, that when a human being
is born, all rejoice; but when he dies, all grieve. It
should be the other way around. No one can tell what
troubles await the developing child on its journey
through life. But when a man has lived well and dies in
peace, all should rejoice, for he has completed his
journey successfully and he is departing from this
world with the imperishable crown of a good name.

ॐ When the child is formed in its mother's womb there
are three partners concerned with it, namely: the Holy
One, blessed be He, the father, and the mother. The
father provides the white semen, from which are
formed the white substances (of the embryo)—the
brain, the nails, the white of the eyes, the bones, and
sinews. The mother provides the red element, from
which are formed the blood, skin, flesh, hair, and the
black in the eyes. The Holy One, may His name be
blessed and His memorial exalted, gives him ten things,
namely: spirit and soul, beauty of features, sight of the
eyes, hearing of the ears, speech of the lips, the ability
to raise the hands and to walk with the feet, wisdom
and understanding, counsel, knowledge, and strength.

When its time comes to die, the Holy One, blessed be
He, takes His portion and leaves the portion contrib-
uted by the father and mother before them, and they
weep. The Holy One, blessed be He, says to them:
"Why do you weep? Have I taken anything of yours? I
have only taken what belongs to Me!" They say before
Him, "Lord of the universe, so long as Thy portion was
mingled with ours, our portion was preserved from the

maggot and worm; but now that Thou hast taken away Thy portion from ours, behold our portion is cast away and given to the maggot and worm."

✎ Moses wanted to inform his brother of his impending death, but knew not how to go about it. At length he said to him: "Aaron, my brother, hath God given anything into thy keeping?" "Yes," replied Aaron. "What, pray?" asked Moses. Aaron: "The altar and the table upon which is the shewbread hath He given into my charge." Moses: "It may be that He will now demand back from thee all that He hath given into thy keeping." Aaron: "What, pray?" Moses: "Hath He not entrusted a light to thee?" Aaron: "Not one light only but all seven of the candlesticks that now burn in the sanctuary."

Moses had, of course, intended to call Aaron's attention to the soul, "the light of the Lord," which God had given into his keeping and which He now demanded back. As Aaron, in his simplicity, did not notice the allusion, Moses did not go into further particulars, but remarked to Aaron: "God hath with justice called thee an innocent, simple-hearted man."

✎ Rabbi Meir sat during the whole of one Sabbath day in the public school and instructed the people. During his absence from his house, his two sons, both of uncommon beauty and enlightened in the law, died. His wife bore them to her bedchamber, laid them upon the marriage bed, and spread a white covering over their bodies.

Toward evening Rabbi Meir came home. "Where are my beloved sons," he asked, "that I may give them my blessing?" "They are gone to the school," was the answer. "I repeatedly looked round the school," he replied, "and I did not see them there." She handed him a goblet; he praised the Lord at the going out of the Sabbath, drank, and again asked, "Where are my sons, that they may drink of the cup of blessing?" "They will not be far off," she said, and placed food before him, that he might eat.

He was in a gladsome and genial mood, and when he had said grace after the meal, she thus addressed him: "Rabbi, with thy permission, I would propose to thee one question." "Ask it then, my love!" he replied. Said she, "A few days ago, a person entrusted some jewels to my custody, and now he demands them again. Should I give them back?" "This is a question," said Rabbi Meir, "which my wife should not have thought it necessary to ask. What! would you hesitate or be reluctant to restore to everyone his own?" "No," she replied, "but yet I thought it best not to restore them without acquainting you therewith."

She then led him to their chamber and, stepping to the bed, took the white covering from the bodies. The father cried: "Ah, my sons! my sons! the light of mine eyes, and the light of my understanding; I was your father, but you were my teachers in the law!"

The mother turned away and wept bitterly. At length she took her husband by the hand and said: "My husband and my Rabbi, did you not teach me that we must not be reluctant to restore that which was entrusted to our keeping? See, the Lord gave, the Lord has taken away, and blessed be the name of the Lord!" "Blessed be the name of the Lord!" echoed Rabbi Meir, "and blessed be His name for your sake too! for well is it written, 'He that hath found a virtuous woman hath a greater treasure than costly pearls. She openeth her mouth with wisdom; and the law of kindness is on her tongue'" (Proverbs 31:26).

THE ACQUISITIVENESS OF MAN

❧ Rabbi Meir taught: When man enters this world his fists are clenched tight, as if to say: "The world is mine. I shall soon hold it all within the grasp of my hand."

When he leaves this world, his palms are wide open, as if to declare: "I have not inherited a thing from the world."

The moral of the preceding story is apparent. Man thinks to conquer the world and hold its possessions in his hands. God has ordained that he may not carry any of his material possessions with him into the "great beyond." Therefore, let man be charitable and ever share his possessions with others.

❧ The fox once came upon a vineyard that was fenced in by a solid wall. There was but one opening in that wall, too narrow for a fox to shove through and get into the vineyard. So the fox decided to reduce the size of his body by abstaining from food for a few days. When he had made his way into the vineyard he proceeded to regain his former strength and size by eating of the grapes. After a time he wished to leave the vineyard, but discovered that he was too large for the narrow exit. So once again he had to resort to fasting. Weak and emaciated, he finally emerged on the other side of the wall, and by way of farewell he spoke these words: "Vineyard, O vineyard, thou art beautiful and thy fruit is sweet, yet of what benefit art thou to one who must leave thee in the same condition as he was when he entered thee?"

❧ Pursuing his way through dreary deserts in search of victory and spoil, Alexander the Great came at last to a rivulet. Overcome by fatigue and hunger, he was obliged to stop. He seated himself on the riverbank and took a draught of water. He then ordered some salt fish to be brought to him. These he dipped in the steam to remove the briny taste, and was much surprised to find them emit a very fine fragrance. "Surely," said he, "this river, which possesses such uncommon qualities, must flow from a very rich and happy country. Let us march thither."

Following the course of the river, he at length arrived at the gates of paradise. He knocked and, with his usual impetuosity, demanded admittance.

"Thou canst not be admitted here!" exclaimed a voice from within; "this gate is the Lord's." "I am the Lord—the lord of the earth," answered the impatient chief. "I am Alexander the Conqueror!" The voice replied, "Here, we know of no conquerors—save such as conquer their passions: none but the just can enter here."

Seeing all his attempts fruitless, Alexander addressed himself to the guardian of paradise: "You know I am a great king, who receives the homage of nations. At least give me something that I may show to an astonished and admiring world when I return." "Here, madman!" said the guardian of paradise, "here is something for thee. One glance at it may teach thee more wisdom than thou hast hitherto derived from all thy instructors. Now go thy way."

Alexander took the gift and returned to his tent. But what was his confusion to discover that it was a fragment of a human skull!

"And is this," exclaimed Alexander, "the mighty gift that they bestow on kings and heroes?" Enraged and disappointed, he threw it on the ground.

"Great king!" said a learned man who happened to be present, "do not despise this gift. Despicable as it appears in thine eyes, it yet possesses some extraordinary qualities, of which thou mayest soon be convinced, if thou wilt order it to be weighed against gold or silver."

Alexander ordered it to be done, and to the astonishment of the beholders, the skull overbalanced the gold. As more gold was put in the one scale, the lower sank that which contained the skull. "Strange!" exclaimed Alexander, "that so small a portion of matter should outweigh so large a mass of gold! Is there nothing that will counterbalance it?"

Then the philosophers covered the fragment with some earth, and immediately down went the gold, and the opposite scale ascended. "This is most extraordinary!" exclaimed Alexander. "Great king," said the sages, "this fragment is the socket of the human eye, which, though small in compass, is yet unbounded in its desire. Neither gold nor silver nor any other earthly possession can ever satisfy it. But when it once is laid in the grave and covered with a little earth, there is an end to its lust and ambition."

Jewish tradition has insisted that simple wooden coffins without ornamentation must be used for the burial of the dead. Likewise all are to be garbed in white shrouds, and it is forbidden to adorn the corpse with finery or expensive garments. This is to teach that the prince and the pauper, the rich and the poor, the wise and the simple, are all equal in death.

RESISTANCE TO DEATH

"The will to live" that God has breathed into us compels man to cling to life and resist death. According to the

*following story, even such a one as Moses was reluctant to
depart from this world and to yield his soul to God:*

🐉 God was angry with Moses because he would not
resign himself to death, but His wrath vanished when
Moses spoke these words: "The Lord, the Lord, a God
full of compassion and gracious, slow to anger, and
plenteous in mercy and truth; keeping mercy for thousands, forgiving iniquity and transgression and sin."

God now said kindly to Moses: "I have made two
vows, one that thou art to die, and the second that
Israel is to perish. I cannot cancel both vows. If thou
choosest to live, then Israel must perish."

"Lord of the universe!" replied Moses, "Thou seizest
the rope at both ends, so that now I must say, 'Rather
shall Moses and a thousand like him die, than a single
soul out of Israel!' But will not all men exclaim, 'Alas!
The feet that trod the heavens, the face that beheld the
face of the Divine Glory, and the hands that received
the Torah, shall not enter the grave!'"

God replied: "Nay, the people will say: 'If a man such
as Moses, who ascended into heaven, who beheld the
glory of God, and to whom God gave the Torah—if
such a man cannot justify himself before God, how
much less then can an ordinary mortal of flesh and
blood?' I want to know," He added, "why thou canst
not resign thyself to thy impending death."

Moses said: "I fear the sword of the Angel of Death."

God replied: "If this be the reason, then say no more,
for I will not deliver thee into his hand."

Moses, however, would not yield but furthermore
said, "Shall my mother Jochebed, to whom my life
brought grief, suffer sorrow after my death also?"

God answered: "So is the way of the world; every
generation has its scholars, every generation has its

leaders, every generation has its guides. Heretofore, it was thy duty to lead the people, but now thy disciple Joshua will relieve thee of the office destined for him."

When Moses perceived that all things in heaven and earth were deaf to his entreaty, he begged mankind to intercede for him before God. He went first to his successor Joshua, saying: "O my son, be mindful of my love for thee, how I taught thee mishnah and halachah, and all arts and sciences. Implore God's mercy on my behalf, for perhaps through thee He may yet relent and allow me to enter the land of Israel."

Joshua began to weep bitterly, but when he started to pray, Samael (the Angel of Death) appeared and stopped his mouth, saying, "Why dost thou seek to oppose the command of God, who is 'the Rock, whose work is perfect, and all whose ways are judgment'?" Joshua then went to Moses and, weeping bitterly, said, "Master, Samael will not let me pray." At these words Moses, too, burst into loud sobs.

Samael now approached Moses, saying, "Either I shall kill him or he shall kill me." But Moses arose in anger, and with his staff in his hand, upon which was engraved the Ineffable Name, he went forward to meet the Angel of Death. Samael fled in terror, but Moses pursued him. When Moses reached him, he struck him with his staff, blinded him with the radiance of his face, and then let him run on, overcome with shame and confusion. Then a voice spoke from heaven, "Let him live, Moses, for the world is in need of him."

Moses said: "O Lord of the world! How often did Israel sin before Thee, and when I implored mercy for them, Thou forgavest them, but me Thou wilt not forgive!"

God replied: "The punishment that is laid upon the community is different from the punishment that is laid upon the individual, for I am not so severe in dealing with the community as in dealing with an individual. But know, furthermore, that until now fate had been in thy power, but now fate is no longer in thy power."

Then Moses pleaded: "O Lord of the world! Rise up from the throne of justice, and seat Thyself upon the throne of mercy, so that Thou mayest grant me life, during which to atone for my sins. Deliver me not to the Angel of Death. If Thou wilt grant my prayer, then shall I sound Thy praises to all the inhabitants of the earth; I do not wish to die, 'but live, and declare the works of the LORD'" (Psalm 118:17).

God replied: "'This is the gate of the LORD; the righteous shall enter into it,' this is the gate into which the righteous must enter as well as other creatures, for death hath been decreed for man since the beginning of the world."

When Moses heard these words, he permitted his soul to depart, saying: "Return unto thy rest, O my soul; for the Lord hath dealt bountifully with thee." God thereupon took Moses' soul by kissing him upon the mouth.

The rabbi of Ger said: "Why is man afraid of dying? For does he not then go to his Father! What man fears is the moment he will survey from the other world all the sins he has committed, and the good works he has failed to do on this earth."

THE ETERNAL MYSTERY

The rabbis were not being morbid when they taught that a man should prepare for his death by a lifetime of holiness and goodness. Why, then, are the righteous sometimes taken from this earth before their time? The following story explains the death of the righteous:

✡ Rabbi Hiyya and his disciples were accustomed to rise early and sit under a certain fig tree, the owner of which used to rise early to gather its fruit. Said the disciples: "Perhaps he may suspect us of taking his fruit; let us change our place." Accordingly they changed their place. The owner then went to them and said: "My teachers! This one merit that ye had conferred upon me by sitting and studying under my fig tree—ye have now deprived me of it." "We thought perhaps you suspected us of theft," they replied. But he reassured them, and they returned to their original places. What did he do? The owner did not gather its fruit in the morning, whereupon the figs became wormy. Said the teachers: "The owner of the fig tree knows when the fruit is ripe for plucking, and he plucks it." In the same way, the Holy One, blessed be He, knows when the time of the righteous has come, whereupon He removes them. What is the proof? "My beloved is gone down to his garden" (Song of Songs 6:2).

✡ When Rabbi Bun b. R. Hiyya died, Rabbi Zera went in and delivered a funeral oration over him on the present verse, "Sweet is the sleep of a laboring man." To whom was Rabbi Bun b. R. Hiyya like? To a king who possessed a vineyard and hired many laborers to work it. Among them was one laborer far more skillful in his work than the rest; so what did the king do? He took him by the hand and walked with him up and down. Toward evening the laborers came to receive their wages and this laborer with them, and the king gave him the full amount. The others began to grumble, saying, "We toiled all the day, whereas this man toiled for two hours, and yet the king has given him his full wage!" The king said to them, "What cause have you for grumbling? This man in two hours did more good work than you in a whole day."

Who can presume to fully comprehend the will of God, or question Divine wisdom? One meets the test of faith when he accepts the decisions of God even though they may appear to be devoid of justice and mercy.

Those who are righteous receive their reward through the joy that derives from obedience to God. Although it appears to mortal men that God has summoned them too early, it is only because we cannot understand Divine providence. The Midrash teaches that "tombstones need not be erected for the righteous, because their teachings and their deeds are their memorials." By bringing men closer to God they have made a contribution that is inestimable. How is it possible then for us to say whether their life has been long or short when assessed by the calendar of divinity? "Furthermore," say the rabbis, "we measure a life by heartthrobs, and not by the ticking of a clock or by years."

PREPARING FOR ETERNAL LIFE

We prepare for eternal life by our thoughts and deeds. Man must learn to value time and use the years as precious gifts of God. He must know that life is fleeting, and therefore, it is incumbent upon him to use the few years that are his for holiness, beauty, goodness, and love.

A student of Rabbi Yerahmiel once came into the master's room and found him lying down and playing with his watch. He was surprised because it was almost noon and the rabbi had not yet prayed. Just then Rabbi Yerahmiel said to the Hasid: "You are surprised at what I am doing? But do you really know what I am doing? I am learning how to leave the world."

The psalmist reminds us of the brevity of life with the admonition "So teach us to number our days, that we may get us a heart of wisdom" (Psalm 90:12).

⅋ King David summoned the court jeweler before him, saying: "Make for me a ring and inscribe upon it a statement that will enable me to modulate my happiness when I experience an excess of triumph. But, hear ye, the same inscription must also lift me up when I descend to the depths of despair."

The court jeweler, informed that he would be rewarded if he succeeded, left the king to ponder over the inscription. In time, he made a ring of exceptional beauty, but his efforts to find the required inscription were in vain. As the day approached when he was to appear before King David, the jeweler walked to and fro near the palace garden, wondering what punishment would be meted out to him for his failure.

It was then that the youthful Solomon approached. Throwing himself at the young man's feet, the jeweler wept as he asked: "What can I possibly inscribe upon a ring that will modulate the king's ecstasy and at the same time lift him up when he falls despondent?"

"Inscribe upon the ring," said Solomon, "these words: '*Gam Zeh Ya-avor*' ('This, too, shall pass!'). When the king will gaze upon it in triumph it will reduce his pride. When he will behold it in despair, it will lift up his countenance."

⅋ "And the living will lay it to his heart." What has this verse of Ecclesiastes to teach? Do a kindness that one may be done to you. Attend a funeral that people should attend your funeral; mourn for others so that others should mourn for you; bury so that others should concern themselves with your burial; act benevolently so that benevolence should be done to you.

🦌 "Let thy garments be always white; and let thy head lack no oil" (Ecclesiastes 9:8).

Rabbi Johanan b. Zakkai said: "If the text speaks of white garments, how many of these have the peoples of the world; and if it speaks of good oil, how much of it do the peoples of the world possess! Behold, it speaks only of precepts, good deeds, and Torah."

Rabbi Judah ha-Nasi said: "To what may this be likened? To a king who made a banquet to which he invited guests. He said to them, 'Go, wash yourselves, brush up your clothes, anoint yourselves for the banquet,' but he fixed no time when they were to come to it. The wise among them walked about by the entrance of the king's palace, saying, 'Does the king's palace lack anything?' The foolish among them paid no regard or attention to the king's command. They said, 'We will in due course notice when the king's banquet is to take place, because can there be a banquet without labor to prepare it, and company?' So the plasterer went to his plaster, the potter to his clay, the smith to his charcoal, the washer to his laundry. Suddenly the king ordered, 'Let them all come to the banquet.' They hurried the guests, so that some came in their splendid attire and others came in their dirty garments. The king was pleased with the wise ones who had obeyed his command, and also because they had shown honor to the king's palace. He was angry with the fools who had neglected his command and disgraced his palace. The king said, 'Let those who have prepared themselves for the banquet come and eat of the king's meal, but those who have not prepared themselves shall not partake of it.' You might suppose that the latter were simply to depart; but the king continued, 'No, they are not to depart; but the former shall recline and eat and drink, while these shall remain standing, be punished, and look on and be grieved.' "

Bar Kappara and Rabbi Isaac b. Kappara said: "It may be likened to the wife of a royal courier who adorned herself in the presence of her neighbors. They said to her, 'Your husband is away, so for whom do you adorn yourself?' She answered them, 'My husband is a sailor; and if he should chance to have a little spell of favorable wind, he will come quickly and be here standing above my head. So is it not better that he should see me in my glory and not in my ugliness?' "

🐉 A certain man had three friends, two of whom he loved dearly but the other he lightly esteemed. It happened one day that the king commanded his presence at court, at which he was greatly alarmed and wished to procure an advocate. Accordingly he went to the two friends whom he loved. One flatly refused to accompany him; the other offered to go with him as far as the king's gate, but no farther. In his extremity he called upon the third friend, whom he least esteemed, and he not only went willingly with him, but so ably defended him before the king that he was acquitted.

In like manner every man has three friends when death summons him to appear before his Creator. His first friend, whom he loves most—namely, his money—cannot go with him a single step; his second—relations and neighbors—can only accompany him to the grave, but cannot defend him before the Judge; while his third friend, whom he does not highly esteem—his good works—goes with him before the King and obtains his acquittal.

COMFORT IN SORROW

 Rabbi Nahum once said to his disciples: "If we would hang all our sorrows on pegs, and were allowed to choose those we liked best, every one of us would take back his own, for all the rest would seem even more difficult to bear."

 One of the great Jewish preachers, the Dubner Maggid, told of a king who owned a large, beautiful, pure diamond of which he was justly proud, for it had no equal anywhere. One day the diamond accidentally sustained a deep scratch. The king called in the most skilled diamond cutters and offered them a great reward if they could remove the imperfection from his treasured jewel. But none could repair the blemish. The king was sorely distressed.

After some time a gifted lapidary came to the king and promised to make the rare diamond even more beautiful than it had been before the mishap. The king entrusted the precious stone to his care.

With superb artistry the lapidary engraved a lovely rosebud around the imperfection and used the scratch to make the stem.

The Dubner Maggid used this story to teach us that even when our hearts are scratched and torn with grief, we may use the scratches to create a future of beauty and happiness.

The Midrash reminds us that when Jacob, flying from the wrath of his brother Esau, stopped at Haran, he took stones for a pillow and dreamed of a ladder that reached unto heaven. Sometimes the stones of adversity may enable man to convert his grief into ladders reaching upward to God. A sustaining religious faith will enable man to behold the dawn of hope even

*in the night of sorrow. It will enable him to convert his grief
into a triumph of the spirit.*

🎖 As Rabbi Gamaliel, Rabbi Eleazar ben Azariah, Rabbi
Joshua, and Rabbi Akiba were on the way to Rome,
they heard the voice of the crowds at Rome from
Puteoli, 120 miles away. They all began to weep, but
Rabbi Akiba laughed. They said to him: "These heathen
peoples worship idols and live in safety and prosperity,
whereas the Temple of our God is burned down and
has become a dwelling place for the beasts of the field,
so should we not weep?" He said to them, "For that
reason am I merry. If they that offend Him fare thus,
how much better shall they fare that obey Him!"

On another occasion they were coming up to Jerusalem, and when they reached the Temple mount, they
saw a fox emerging from the Holy of Holies. They fell
a-weeping, but Rabbi Akiba laughed. They said to him,
"Akiba, you always surprise us. Shall we not weep that
from the Holy of Holies a fox emerges, and concerning
it the verse is fulfilled, 'For the mountain of Zion, which
is desolate, the foxes walk upon it'?"

He said to them: "For that reason am I merry. Behold
it states, 'And I will take unto Me faithful witnesses to
record, Uriah the priest, and Zechariah the son of
Jeberechiah.' Now Uriah lived in the time of the first
Temple, while Zechariah lived in the time of the second
Temple! But what did Uriah say? 'Thus saith the Lord of
hosts: Zion shall be plowed as a field, and Jerusalem
shall become heaps.' And what did Zechariah say?
'There shall yet old men and old women sit in the broad
places of Jerusalem. . . . And the broad places of the
city shall be full of boys and girls playing.' The Holy
One, blessed be He, said, 'Behold I have these two
witnesses, and if the words of Uriah are fulfilled, the

words of Zechariah will be fulfilled; and if the words of Uriah prove vain the words of Zechariah will prove vain.' I rejoiced because the words of Uriah have been fulfilled and in the future the words of Zechariah will be fulfilled."

Thereupon in these terms did they address him: "Akiba, you have consoled us; may you be comforted by the coming of the herald of the redemption!"

The rabbinic tradition discourages excessive grief. Man must resign himself to the will of God.

🎋 The son of a rabbi mourned the loss of his beloved father. Day after day he went to the cemetery and prostrated himself on the grave of his father. One day as the son gave way to paroxysms of sorrow, his father appeared unto him in a vision and said: "My son, do you think that you honor my memory with your grief? Excessive grief is foolish. Do you think you truly express your love by your mourning? Offer me no tribute of tears. Build for me no monuments of sorrow. Do not weep for me. Live for me! Show your love by obedience to God's commandments, by devotion to your faith, and by service to your fellow man. This is the memorial that truly honors the departed."

After hearing these words, the son lifted himself from his father's grave, and went forth to make of his father's memory a perpetual light to guide him on paths of righteousness and truth.

Chapter VIII

THE WORLD TO COME

A heathen once asked Rabbi Gamaliel: "Where is the soul? Let me behold it!" The rabbi replied: "Thou wishest to know where God dwells, Who is high as the heavens above the earth; tell me then where dwells the soul which is so near?"

The greatest comfort in sorrow is the assurance that the soul, which is eternal and indestructible, returns to God in life everlasting.

In his sorrow, the poet Tennyson asked: "But what am I? An infant crying in the night. An infant crying for the light, and with no language but a cry." When sorrow befalls us, no matter how schooled we may be in the classroom of life, no matter the degree of maturity we have attained, we are as infants crying in the night. Tennyson was wrong, however, when he said that we have "no language but a cry." There is

*the language of faith that speaks to us in accents divine. If we
listen to the "still small voice" of God, then we will be
sustained with the conviction that the soul can never die. If
the soul can never die, then man inherits eternal life.*

IMMORTALITY OF THE SOUL

*The belief in the immortality of the soul is a basic principle
of Judaism. The body, which is of the earth, returns to the
earth. "Dust returneth to dust, but the spirit returneth unto
God who gave it." The traditional prayer of the Jewish
liturgy,* Elohai Neshomo, *attests to this belief:*
*My God, the soul which Thou hast given unto me came
pure from Thee. Thou hast created it, Thou hast formed it,
Thou hast breathed it into me; Thou hast preserved it in this
body and, at the appointed time, Thou wilt take it from this
earth that it may enter upon life everlasting. While the soul
animates my being I will worship Thee, Sovereign of the
world and Lord of all souls. Praised be Thou, O Lord, in
whose hands are the souls of all the living and the spirits of all
flesh.*
*In rabbinic Judaism, in keeping with the Pharisaic tradi-
tion, there are references to the resurrection of the body, but
these statements are not in harmony with the basic, definitive
principle of Judaism that when death comes, the body disin-
tegrates and returns to dust, while the soul continues in life
eternal with God.*
*The following homily is not characteristic of the dominant
tradition of Judaism. It is cited, however, to illustrate the
culpability of both the body and the soul.*

🦌 "The soul and the body can both escape punishment," said Antoninus to Rabbi Judah. "How?" he
asked. Antoninus said: "The body can say: 'The soul

committed the sin, for see, ever since the soul left me, I have been lying in my tomb mute as a stone.' And the soul can say: 'It was the body that committed the sin, for see, ever since I left it I have been flying through space like a bird.' "

To this Rabbi Judah replied: "Let me tell you a parable. To what can this be compared? There was a king who had a beautiful garden wherein grew the loveliest of early fruits. He put two keepers in the garden, and one of them was blind, the other paralytic. One day the paralytic said to his blind companion: 'I see some beautiful fruit: Come, I will climb up on your shoulders, and we will pluck the fruit and eat it.' And the paralytic climbed up on the shoulders of the blind man, and they plucked the fruit and ate it. After a few days the owner of the garden appeared and asked: 'What happened to the beautiful fruit?' The paralytic replied: 'How can I have taken them, I who have no limbs?' And the blind man said: 'How can I have taken them, I who cannot see?' What did the king do? He put the paralytic on the shoulders of the blind man, and he punished them both together. Even so will the Holy One, blessed be He, seek out the soul, put it back in the body, and punish both of them together."

This should be regarded as anomalous to biblical and modern Judaism, which does not emphasize either punishment or reward in the world to come.

LIFE IN THE WORLD TO COME

The Mosaic code and the prophets of Israel apply their promises and threats of reward and punishment to this world,

*nor do they indicate by a single word the belief in a judgment
or a weighing of actions in the world to come.*

*In rabbinic literature, however, there are divergent opin-
ions as to the nature of life in the world to come. Rabbi
Shammai contended that the good dwell with God, the evil go
to Gehinom (comparable to hell), and the intermediate go
down and come up to be healed after a period of time. Rabbi
Hillel disagreed and insisted that God's mercy would not
permit Him to send His children to Gehinom.*

🍂 Rab, a Babylonian teacher of the third century, said:
"The world to come is not like this world. There is no
eating and drinking, no begetting of children, no bar-
gaining, no jealousy, hatred, or strife. The righteous sit
with crowns on their heads. What then will they eat
and drink? The presence of God is food and drink to
them."

🍂 Rabbi Judah gave a banquet in honor of his son, but
he forgot to invite Bar Kappara. The latter wrote over
the rabbi's doorpost: "Death shall come when thy
merriment is ended, and what then will there be to thy
merriment?"

When the rabbi read this and asked who had written
it, he was told: "Bar Kappara, whom you did not
invite."

The following day he gave another banquet, and on
this occasion he invited Bar Kappara. When the dishes
reached his table, Bar Kappara would embark upon the
narration of fables, and the food grew cold. The rabbi
noticed that the servants took back the food from the
table uneaten, and he asked Bar Kappara why he
interrupted the meal with his fables. Bar Kappara
replied: "To show thee that I rebuked thee yesterday,
but not because I was eager for your food."

The rabbi begged his pardon and they were reconciled.

Said Abba Bar Kappara to the rabbi: "If thou enjoyest so much prosperity in the world which is not thine for long, how much more shalt thou enjoy in the world that shall be thine forever!"

What Abba Bar Kappara refers to here is not physical enjoyment or material prosperity, but the happiness that comes from nearness to God. This happiness will be further assured by the mercy and compassion of God.

🦌 "Their Redeemer is strong, the LORD of hosts is His name; He will thoroughly plead their cause" (Jeremiah 50:34).

Daniel the tailor interpreted this verse as referring to the illegitimate. These are the actual illegitimate. Now what wrong has such a person done? A man has illicit intercourse and begets this child. How has the latter sinned and how is he responsible? Rabbi Judah b. Pazzi said: "Even illegitimates enter the world to come; for it is written, 'And behold the tears of such as were oppressed, and they had no comforter.' The Holy One, blessed be He, spake, 'Since they were under a disability in this world, as regards the hereafter.' Zechariah says, 'I will see that they have seats [of pure gold],' " as it is stated, "Behold a candlestick all of gold, with a bowl [gullah] upon the top of it . . . and two olive trees by it!"

This homily is intended to teach compassion for the illegitimate and the handicapped, rather than offer a commentary on life in the hereafter. Nonetheless it indicates that the disabilities of this life will be equitably adjusted in the world to come before a God of infinite mercy.

The Talmud tells of the son of Rabbi Joshua who fell ill, swooned, and was accounted as dead. When he revived, his father asked him what he saw. He said: "I saw a topsy-turvy world."

The "topsy-turvy world" refers to those who may be scorned in this world but are held in great honor in the world to come. The values that are regarded lightly in this world are revered and applied in the world to come.

PUNISHMENT AND REWARD

The mainstream of Jewish thought would discount the belief in punishment and suffering after death. If, as we believe, God is our Heavenly Father, merciful and compassionate, how is it possible for a Father to relegate His children to the suffering and torture of hell in the afterlife? The psalmist's belief that "as a father hath compassion upon his children, so will the LORD have compassion upon us" is the belief of Judaism. Moreover, the constantly repeated refrain of the prayer book, that "God remembers that we are but dust," indicates the hope in God's forgiveness. The Divine Father knows the imperfections and the limitations of His children. He has created man fallible and limited, as flesh and blood human beings, and not angels. Therefore will the Divine judgment be tempered by Divine mercy, even though we have erred and sinned. Just as a father is distressed and grieved because of the sins of his children, so our Heavenly Father is grieved at the sins of man. But, just as a mortal father will forgive his children in love despite the enormity of their sins, so the Lord God transcends hatred and vengeance to forgive His children in love.

The Jew has never feared the afterlife, nor has he been terrorized by threats of eternal punishment. Conversely, he has never anticipated the pleasures of a physical heaven. As death approaches, he recalls the cherished words of the Jewish prayer book:

> Into Thy hands, O God, I commit my
>   soul,
> Both when I wake and when I sleep,
> And with my soul, my body, too.
> The Lord is with me, I shall not fear.

The first line was repeated by Jesus: "And when Jesus had cried with a loud voice, he said, 'Father, into thy hands I commend my spirit'" (Luke 23:46).

⚶ Why does the Jew garb himself in white on the Day of Atonement? ask the rabbis. They answer: It was traditional for the defendant before the bar of judgment to wear black to receive the verdict of guilty, and white to receive the verdict of innocent. So do the children of Israel garb themselves in white, so sure are they of Divine mercy and forgiveness. If God were to hold man accountable for his sins, who could stand before Him? ask the rabbis. It is only because of God's love and mercy that the world endures.

⚶ One day a philosopher said to Rabbi Gamaliel: "It is written in your sacred book: 'The LORD thy God is a devouring fire, a jealous God.' Why is it, then, that He proceeds against the idolaters and not against the idols themselves?" To which Gamaliel replied: "If the pagans adored such things as the world did not need, God would surely destroy them; but see, they worship the sun, the moon, the stars, the planets, the springs, and the valleys; shall He, because of these, destroy all of His beautiful universe?"

If God were a jealous God, then not only idolaters, but even the children of Israel, could not live because of their disobedience of the Divine commandments.

⚜ When Moses saw that God wrote the word "long-suffering" in the Torah, he asked: "Does this mean that Thou hast patience with the pious?" But God answered: "Nay, with sinners also am I long-suffering." "What!" exclaimed Moses. "Let the sinners perish!" God said no more, but when Moses implored God's mercy, begging Him to forgive the sins of the people of Israel, God answered him: "Thou thyself didst advise Me to have no patience with sinners and to destroy them." "Yea," said Moses, "but Thou didst declare that Thou art long-suffering with sinners also; let now the patience of the Lord be great according as Thou hast spoken."

It is clear that the concept of physical suffering in a physical hell is alien to Jewish religious thought. It is likewise manifest that the hedonistic concept of heaven with the satisfaction of material appetites is also contrary to Jewish religious thought. The greatest hell is removal from God. The most exalted heaven is the nearness of God. Heaven, therefore, is not a place, but a Divine state of being accorded to God's children.

⚜ Once Rabbi Shneur Zalman interrupted his prayers and said: "I do not want Your paradise. I do not want Your coming world. I want You, O God, and You only!" To have the love of God is to possess the heaven of all heavens.

⚜ Even on his deathbed, the Baal Shem too said: "All my life I have been wanting to give gifts to God. I have but two hours more to live. What, then, shall I give

Thee, O God? I therefore make God a gift of those two hours." The Baal Shem was then summoned on high two hours before the appointed time of his death.

🦌 Will there be immortality for non-Jews? Rabbi Joshua replied emphatically: "The righteous of all the nations (and religions) of the earth have a share in the world to come."

Although there are instances in the Talmud where some rabbis express the view that only the righteous of Israel have a share in the world to come, the preponderant opinion of the majority is that since God is the Heavenly Father and has created all men in His image, therefore the righteous of all peoples and all nations share in God's love, and consequently, in the world to come.

Repudiating the concept of the immortality of the body, Judaism cleaves to the sacred belief in the immortality of the soul. If there is no body, then there can be no physical hell. With no body that may be tortured, the very thought of physical suffering in an afterlife seems patently illogical and untenable. It is the immortal soul that ascends to God. Since the soul is incorporeal and without substance or form, then the soul may not be subject to physical pain or suffering. Reason and faith combine to assure those of the Jewish faith that the soul, the portion of divinity within man, becomes one with the Holy God, the Divine source of all life, in this world and in the world to come.

Since finite man is limited in his understanding, he is not endowed with the ability to comprehend the infinity of God or the nature of the world to come. There are dangers attendant to the presumptuous inquiry of man into the mystery of the hereafter.

🦌 Four rabbis determined to enter paradise to resolve the mystery of the hereafter. Because of their holiness, they were able to rise above the earth to a heavenly dimension. Rabbi Ben Assai gazed upon the mystery and died. Rabbi Ben Zoma became demented. Rabbi Acher lost his faith and became an apostate. Only Rabbi Akiba knew how to walk in the paradise of mystical speculation and return to earth without losing his life, his reason, or his faith. Here the punishment for "storming the towers of heaven" is in this world.

Accordingly, it may be asked: If there is no heaven or hell in the world to come, how are the wicked punished and the righteous rewarded? The emphasis in Jewish thought is Divine retribution that applies to this world. Man receives his reward and punishment on earth—although it may not be at the time or in the way that he anticipates. Believing that "goodness engenders goodness, and evil engenders evil," Judaism teaches that goodness is its own reward, and that evil brings evil as an inevitable consequence of sinful deeds or thoughts. Goodness is the joy of living in the presence of God. Evil causes one to depart from the presence of God. To the rabbis, there could be no greater reward or punishment.

The rabbinic concept of retribution insists that just as there are evil consequences that derive from the breaking of the physical laws of nature, so there are evil consequences that derive from disobedience to the moral laws of God. A man should seek goodness and not evil, without consideration of reward, because man is created in the Divine image which places upon him the obligation of morality. It is for this reason that repentance is so essential.

✄ "God waits until the hour of man's death, hoping that he will repent of his evil ways." The rabbis taught: "Repent one day before thy death." Since no man has the prescience to know the day of his death, "let him repent today. It may be the day before his death."

🦌 Once the Baal Shem Tov ordered Rabbi Zev Kitzes to learn the secret meanings behind the blasts of the ram's horn, because Rabbi Zev was to be his caller on Rosh Hashanah (the New Year).

Having studied the secret meanings, Rabbi Zev copied them on a piece of paper to glance at during the service. He then placed the paper in his bosom. When the time arrived for the blowing of the ram's horn, he searched frantically for his notes, but to no avail. Therefore, he did not know on what meanings to concentrate. Brokenhearted, he wept bitterly and called the blasts of the ram's horn, without meditating on the secret meanings involved.

Afterward the Baal Shem Tov said to him: "Lo, in the habitation of the king are to be found many rooms and apartments, and there is a key for each lock; but the master key is the ax, with which it is possible to open all the locks on all the doors. Thus it is with the ram's horn: The secret meanings are the keys; every gate has a different meaning, but the master key is the broken heart. When a man sincerely breaks his heart before God in repentance, he can enter into all the gates of the apartments of the King of all Kings."

🦌 The rabbis taught that it is never too late to repent and return to God. "Thou wilt return to the Lord thy God." Rabbi Samuel Pargrita said, in the name of Rabbi Meir: "This can be compared to the son of a king who took to evil ways. The king sent a tutor to him, who appealed to him, saying, 'Repent, my son.' The son, however, sent him back to his father with the message, 'How can I have the effrontery to return? I am ashamed to come before you.' Thereupon his father sent back word, 'My son, is a son ever ashamed to return to his father? And is it not to your father that you will be

returning?' Similarly, the Holy One, blessed be He, sent
Jeremiah to Israel when they sinned, and said to him:
'Go, say to My children, Return.' Whence this? For it is
said, 'Go, and proclaim these words . . .' (Jeremiah
3:12). Israel asked Jeremiah: 'How can we have the
effrontery to return to God?' Whence do we know this?
For it is said, 'Let us lie down in our shame, and let our
confusion cover us' (Jeremiah 3:25). But God sent word
back to them: 'My children, if you return, will you not
be returning to your Father?' "

Rabbi Simeon ben Lakish and two companions, in
their younger days, were robbers. Rabbi Simeon repented and became a man of great piety and learning.
His companions, however, held to their evil ways.

It happened that the three died on the same day.
Rabbi Simeon was led to paradise, but his former
comrades were taken to Gehinom. They complained:
"But we were together in our robberies." They received
answer: "But Simeon repented and you did not."

"We are ready, however, to repent now," they said.
The answer was given: "He who travels through a
desert must take along his food lest he starve. He who
travels at sea must carry provisions lest he be hungry.
The afterlife is like both the desert and the sea, and no
provisions can be obtained there."

Wisdom was asked: "The sinner, what of his punishment?" Said she to those who asked: "The soul that
sinneth, it shall die" (Ezekiel 18:20).

The Torah was asked: "The sinner, what of his
punishment?" Said she to those who asked: "Let him
bring a guilt offering and he will be atoned for" (Leviticus 1:4).

The Holy One, blessed be He, was asked: "The

sinner, what of his punishment?" Said He to those who asked: "Let him repent and he will be atoned for; as it is said, 'Good and upright is the LORD; therefore doth He instruct sinners in the way' " (Psalm 25:8).

"My children, what do I beseech of you," says God, "but to seek Me and live!"

A king's son was at a distance of a hundred days' journey from his father. Said his friends to him, "Return to your father."

He said to them, "I cannot. The way is too far."

His father sent to him and said, "Go as far as you are able and I shall come the rest of the way to you."

Thus the Holy One, blessed be He, said to Israel: "Return unto Me, and I will return unto you" (Malachi 3:7).

Rabbi Jacob taught: "This world is like a vestibule before the world to come. Prepare thyself in the vestibule, that thou mayest enter into the hall." He used to say: "Better is one hour of repentance and good deeds in this world than the whole life of the world to come. However, better is one hour of the blissfulness of spirit in the world to come, than the whole life of this world."

An angel once disobeyed God, and, summoned before the throne of judgment, the angel begged for mercy. God said, "I shall not punish you, but in atonement for your sin you must return to earth and bring back for Me the most precious thing in the world."

The angel flew down to earth and traversed hills and valleys, seas and rivers, in search of the most precious thing in the world. Finally after a number of years, the angel came upon a battlefield and beheld a brave soldier dying of the wounds he had received in defense of his country. The angel seized a drop of blood and brought it to the throne of glory, and said, "Lord God, surely this is the most precious thing in the world." God said, "Indeed, O angel, this is precious in My sight, but it is not the most precious thing in the world."

And so the angel returned to earth and, after many years of wandering, came to a hospital where a nurse lay dying of a dread disease that she had contracted through nursing others. As the last breath passed from her lifeless form, the angel caught it up and brought it to the throne of judgment, saying "O Lord God, surely this is the most precious thing in the world." God smiled at the angel and said, "Indeed, O angel, sacrifice in behalf of others is precious, but go once again and bring back to Me the most precious thing in the world."

The angel returned to the earth and this time wandered for many years, and then it happened that the angel beheld a villainous looking man riding through the dark forest. He was armed with sword and buckler, spear and arrows. He was going to the hut of his enemy to destroy him. As he approached the enemy's house, light streamed from the windows, and the members of the household, unsuspecting, went about their tasks. The villain approached and looked into the window. There he saw the wife putting the little son to bed, teaching him to pray, instructing him to thank God for all His blessings. As the villainous man looked at this scene, he forgot why he had come. He remembered his own childhood—how his mother had put him to bed and taught him to pray to God. The man's heart melted and a tear rolled down his cheek. The angel caught the tear and flew and returned to heaven to God, saying, "Dear Lord, surely this is the most precious thing in the world—the tear of repentance."

God beamed upon the angel as he spoke, "Indeed, O angel, you have brought Me the most precious thing in the world. Repentance opens the gates of heaven. It is indeed most precious in My sight."

THE RIGHTEOUS AND THE WORLD TO COME

It is taught in the Midrash that the righteous will inherit the light and peace of the world to come. The following homilies indicate the teachings of the rabbis in this regard:

🦋 When the righteous wish to dwell in tranquility in this world, Satan comes and accuses them: They are not content with what is in store for them in the hereafter, but they wish to dwell at ease even in this world! The proof lies in the fact that the patriarch Jacob wished to live at ease in this world, whereupon he was beset with troubles.

🦋 Rabbi Alexandri said: "There is no man without suffering: Happy is he whose sufferings come because of his obedience to God's commandments."

Rabbi Judah, seeing a blind man engaged in the study of the Torah, greeted him with these words, "Peace to thee, thou free man." "Have you then heard that I was formerly a slave?" he exclaimed. "No," answered Rabbi Judah, "but I mean that because of your suffering in this world you will be a free man in the hereafter."

🦋 Rabbi Simeon ben Lakish said: "Every righteous man has a world for himself in the hereafter. What is the proof? 'Because man goeth to the home of his world' (Ecclesiastes 12:5). This may be compared to a king who enters a country accompanied by governors, prefects, and generals. Though they all enter through one gate, each is given quarters as befit his rank. Similarly, though all experience death, each righteous man has a world for himself, and experiences rest in accordance with the degree of his righteousness. What is the proof? 'Because man goeth to the home of his world.'

"Why was death decreed against the righteous? Because as long as the righteous live they must fight against their evil desires, but when they die they enjoy rest; that is the meaning of 'And there the weary are at rest' (Job 3:17)."

✻ "The sun also ariseth, and the sun goeth down" (Ecclesiastes 1:5). Rabbi Berakiah said: "Do we not know that the sun riseth and sets! What it means, however, is that before the sun of one righteous man sets, He causes the sun of another righteous man to rise. On the day that Moses died, Joshua assumed leadership. On the day that Rabbi Akiba died, Rabbi Judah was born."

✻ Rabbi Simeon ben Lakish also taught: "The days of the righteous die, but they themselves do not die. It does not say: 'And David drew near to die,' but 'Now the days of David drew near to die' (I Kings 2:1); not 'And the Lord said unto Moses: Behold, thou hast drawn near to die'; but, 'Behold thy days have drawn near to die' (Deuteronomy 31:14); not, 'And Israel drew near to die,' but 'and the days of Israel drew near to die.' This is to teach us that days may die, but the righteous never die. They live on forever through their words and through their deeds."

✻ On one occasion the sages asserted that Solomon must surely be excluded from the world to come. A figure with the features of David came and prostrated itself beseechingly before them, but they paid no attention to it. A fire came out from the interior of the Holy of Holies, but they paid no attention to it. A heavenly voice went forth and said: "The man who gave priority to My house over his own, and moreover built My house in seven years while he took thirteen years for his own, should be respected, and such a one shall not stand before mean men."

It is to be noted that Solomon built the Temple of God before he built his own palace.

🦁 Will God be with the righteous in the hereafter? Israel says to the Holy One, blessed be He: "Can the master of the house make a feast for his visitors and not sit down to table with them? Or shall a bridegroom prepare a feast for his guests and not sit down with them?" God answers: "Behold, I will do as you ask."

🦁 Israel is compared to the sand. Just as the sand is trod upon and enables man to advance from one place to another, so Israel through its sufferings, enables man to advance toward God. When referring to the hereafter, however, Israel is compared to the stars. As the stars sparkle throughout the firmament, so will they sparkle in the hereafter; as it is said: "And they that are wise shall shine as the brightness of the firmament; and they that turn the many to righteousness as the stars for ever and ever" (Daniel 12:3). Hence, we know that what applies to Israel applies to all the righteous of the peoples of the world. So will they sparkle in the hereafter.

🦁 The entire reward of the righteous is kept ready for them for the hereafter, and God shows them while yet in this world the reward He is to give them in the future; their souls are then satisfied and they fall asleep forever. Rabbi Eleazar said: "This may be compared to a banquet arranged by a king, who invited the guests and showed them what they would eat and drink, whereby their souls were satisfied, and they fell asleep happily. So does God show the righteous while yet in this world the reward which He is to give them in the future, and thus they fall asleep with satisfied souls. What is that reward? It is the reward of righteous service—the nearness of God."

The rabbis taught: "A banquet will be prepared for the righteous in the world to come." Since rabbinic tradition has already indicated that "just as angels neither eat nor drink, so man does neither eat nor drink in the world to come," how is this to be interpreted? The terms "eat" and "drink" are not to be taken literally. The expression "to drink of the living waters of God," and the teaching that the pious fill themselves to satiety with the word of God, are clues to the suggested meaning.

The following story is consistent with the rabbinic tradition and graphically illustrates the meaning of the teaching "A banquet will be prepared for the righteous in the world to come":

A righteous man was permitted by God to attain foreknowledge of the world to come. In a celestial palace he was ushered into a large room, where he beheld people seated at a banquet table. The table was laden with the most delectable foods, but not a morsel had been touched. The righteous man gazed in wonder at the people seated at the table, because they were emaciated with hunger and they moaned constantly for food, even though the delicious viands were before them.

"If they are hungry, why is it that they don't partake of the food that is before them?" asked the righteous one of his heavenly guide. "They cannot feed themselves," said the guide. "If you will notice, each one has his arms strapped straight, so that no matter how he tries, he cannot get the food into his mouth." "Truly, this is hell," said the righteous one as they left the hall.

The heavenly attendant escorted him across the hall into another room, and the righteous one observed another table equally as beautiful, and laden with delicacies and delectable food. Here he noticed that those seated around the table were well fed, happy, and joyous. To his amazement he discerned that these people, too, had their arms strapped straight. Turning to his guide he asked in perplexity: "How is it then that they are so well fed, seeing that they are unable to transport the food to their mouths?" "Behold," said the heavenly guide. The righteous one looked and he beheld that each one was feeding the other. "In truth," he exclaimed, "this is really heaven!" "In truth it is," agreed the attendant. "As you can see, the difference between hell and heaven is a matter of cooperation and serving one's fellow."

By means of a unique application of biblical exegesis, the rabbis teach that one's immortality is enhanced by his children.

🎜 Rabbi Phinhas bar Hama asked: "What is the meaning of the scriptural verse (I Kings 11:21): 'And when Hadad heard in Egypt that David slept with his fathers, and that Joab the captain of the host was dead . . .'? Why, in the case of David, is it written 'slept,' and, in the case of Joab, 'was dead'?" He answered, "David, who left a son like him, concerning him is said 'slept'; Joab, who left not a son like him, concerning him is said 'was dead.' "

The immortality of the righteous is not only everlasting life in the world to come, but righteous children also assure one's immortality on earth.

Another means of perpetuating oneself is by means of the merit of a good name.

When Rabbi Johanan concluded the book of Job he said thus: "The end of man is death, and the end of cattle is slaughter, and everything is designated for death. Blessed is he that has been reared in the Torah and whose work is in the Torah, and acts so as to please his Creator, and has grown up with a good name, and departed life with a good name. Concerning him, Solomon said: 'A good name is better than precious oil; and the day of death than the day of one's birth' (Ecclesiastes 7:1)."

Humility is regarded as a requisite for the righteous. In this regard the Talmud records a message that was sent from Palestine: "Who is the one that has a share in the world to come? The forbearing and the humble; he who bends his head while entering the house, and bends his head while leaving, always studies the Torah, without taking credit to himself."

Good deeds are vital in helping man earn eternal life.

When man leaves this world, neither silver nor gold nor precious stones nor pearls escort him, but only Torah and good deeds, as it is said: "When thou walkest, it shall lead thee, when thou liest down, it shall watch over thee; and when thou wakest, it shall talk with thee" (Proverbs 6:22). What does this mean? When thou walkest, it shall lead thee—in this world. When thou liest down, it shall watch over thee—in the grave; and when thou wakest, it shall talk with thee—in the future world.

The flame of eternal life burns in the souls of men. The greatest hope is everlasting rest in the presence of a God of love.

⚜ Rab Nachman and Rabbi Isaac were dining together. Said Rab Nachman to Rabbi Isaac: "Tell me something of Torah." Said he: "I heard Rabbi Johanan say that our patriarch Jacob did not die." "What?" asked his disciples in surprise. "Were there not eulogists who eulogized, embalmers who embalmed, and buriers who buried him?" Said he: "I merely interpret this verse: 'Fear thou not, O Jacob, My servant, saith the LORD; neither be dismayed, O Israel; for, lo, I will save thee from afar, and thy seed from the land of their captivity' (Jeremiah 30:10). I compare Jacob to his seed: his seed are alive, and so is he."

By such homiletical exegesis the rabbis assured themselves that Israel lives on forever.

⚜ When a righteous man dies, taught Rabbi Eliezer, three sections of angels come out to greet him. One calls, "He enters into peace"; another calls, "One that walks in his righteousness"; and the other, "They repose on their resting places."

Said Rabbi Hiyya bar Gamda: "When the righteous leaves this world, the ministering angels say to the Holy One, praised be He: 'Such and such a righteous man is coming.' He replies to them: 'Let the righteous come and go out to meet him, and thus say to him, 'He entereth into peace, they rest in their beds' (Isaiah 57:2)."

Rab Hisda was engaged in the study of the Torah day and night, almost without interruption, and his daughter asked him: "My learned father! dost thou not require to sleep a bit?" Said he: "Now the long and inevitable days are approaching, when we will have plenty of time to sleep." The rabbi was referring to his imminent death and to the prospect of eternal rest.

"For the living know that they shall die; but the dead know not anything" (Ecclesiastes 9:5). The Talmud interprets this to mean that the "living" are the righteous who live on after death, and the "dead" are the sinners who are dead while still alive.

The story of Choni, the Rip Van Winkle of the Talmud, teaches that death may be welcomed as a blessing.

🐾 One day while walking along the road, Choni saw a man planting a carob tree, and he said to him, "Since a carob tree does not bear fruit for seventy years, how can you be certain of living long enough to eat from it?" The man answered: "I found the world filled with carob trees; as my forefathers planted them for me, I likewise plant them for my descendants." Choni thereupon sat down, had his meal, and fell asleep. While he slumbered, a grotto grew around him so that he was hidden from view. And he slept for seventy years.

On awakening, he saw a man gathering carobs from the very carob tree. Choni asked him, "Do you know who planted this carob tree?" The reply came: "My grandfather." Choni exclaimed, "Surely seventy years have passed like a dream!"

Then he went to his house and inquired whether the

son of Choni the circle-drawer still lived. They told him
that his son was no more, but his grandson was living.
He said to them, "I am Choni," but they would not
believe him. He went to the academy, where he heard
the rabbis say: "Our studies are not as clear as in the
time of Choni the circle-drawer, for when he entered
the academy he used to solve all the difficulties of the
scholars." He said to them, "I am Choni," but they
would not believe him or pay him the honor due him.
Alone, unhappy, without friends or plans for the future, he thereupon prayed to God that he might die,
and he died. Hence arose the proverb, "Either compan-
ionship or death."

HEAVEN ON EARTH

When the rabbis refer to the Olom ha-bo *(the world to
come), they may mean the following: the world after death,
life in paradise or in Gehinom, the life of the soul with God,
the era of the Messiah, or the future life in this world.*

*The troubles and vicissitudes of this life prompted the rabbis
to meditate on whether it would be better not to have been
born.*

For two and a half years the school of Shammai and
the school of Hillel differed. The former said: "It would
have been better for man not to have been born at all
than to have been born." The latter said: "It would have
been better for man to have been born than not to have
been born." Their votes were finally taken, and it was
decided: It would have been better for man not to have
been born at all than to have been born. But since he
has been born, let him investigate his past doings. And
others say: Let him examine what he is doing.

The decision was not as melancholy as it appears to us. Both the schools and the teachers, Shammai and Hillel, taught the worthwhileness of life, and insisted that man must persistently sanctify life with holiness. The conclusion is given cryptically here. The full discussion, however, reveals that the decision to create man was made by God. It is not up to us to question Divine wisdom. Since man has been created, let him evaluate his deeds, repent of his sins, and live in accordance with the moral will of God in this world.

Judaism is primarily a this-wordly religion. Since God, the King of all Kings, rules over the kingdom of heaven, it is incumbent upon man to enter into a copartnership with God to make His kingdom on earth a glorious reality.

There was a sage of unusual virtue and holiness who asked for the privilege of visiting paradise. His wish was granted, and he was transported to paradise, where he saw the sages studying the Torah. He exclaimed: "But they did the same thing on earth!" A heavenly voice answered: "The sages are not in paradise. Paradise is in the sages."

This is not limited to sages. There is a paradise within every child of God. We gain paradise-within through the Divine soul that enables us to quest for truth, justice, goodness, and holiness. Man is compelled by the challenge of God to work for the future and build God's kingdom on earth.

The Emperor Hadrian, passing near Tiberias in Galilee, observed an old man digging a large trench in order to plant some fig trees. "Hadst thou properly employed the morning of thy life," said Hadrian, "thou needest not to have worked so hard in the evening of thy days." "I have well employed my early days, nor will I neglect the evening of my life; and let God do what He thinks best," replied the man. "How old mayest thou be, good man?" asked the emperor. "A hundred years," was the reply. "What," exclaimed Hadrian, "a hundred years old art thou, and still plantest trees! Canst thou, then, hope ever to enjoy the fruits of thy labor?" "Great king," rejoined the hoary-headed man, "yes, I do hope; if God permit, I may even eat the fruit of these very trees; if not, my children will. Have not my forefathers planted trees for me, and shall I not do the same for my children?" Hadrian, pleased with the honest man's reply, said, "Well, old man, if ever thou livest to see the fruit of these trees, let me know it. Dost thou hear, good old man?" And with these words he left him.

The old man did live long enough to see the fruits of his industry. The trees flourished and bore excellent fruit. As soon as they were sufficiently ripe, he gathered the most choice figs, put them in a basket, and marched off toward the emperor's residence. Hadrian happened to look out of one of the windows of his palace. Seeing a man bent with age, with a basket on his shoulders, standing near the gate, he ordered him to be admitted to his presence.

"What is thy pleasure, old man?" demanded Hadrian. "May it please your majesty," replied the man, "to recollect seeing once a very old man planting some trees, and you desired him, if ever he should gather the fruit, to let you know. I am that old man and this is the fruit of those very trees. May it please you graciously to accept them as a humble tribute of gratitude for your majesty's great condescension." Hadrian ordered the basket to be emptied of the fruit, and to be filled with gold, and he gave it to the old man as a present.

Man must constantly direct his efforts to the future, even though the task of building a better world may seem to be insuperable.

THE MESSIAH IDEA IN JUDAISM

"Will man's effort to build a religious future be aided by the Messiah?" The answer to this question requires a brief explanation of the concept of the Messiah in Judaism.

Moses was permitted to converse with the Messiah. "But if thou sayest," said the Messiah, "that God with His own hands builds Himself a Temple in heaven, know then that with His hands also He will build the Temple upon earth."

When Moses heard these words from the mouth of the Messiah, he rejoiced greatly, and lifting up his face to God, he said, "O Lord of the world! When will this Temple built here in heaven come down to earth below?" God replied: "I have made known the time of this event to no creature, either to the earlier ones or to the later. How then should I tell thee?" Moses said: "Give me a sign, so that out of the happenings in the world I may gather when that time will approach." God answered: "I shall first scatter Israel as with a shovel over all the earth, so that they may be scattered among all nations in the four corners of the earth, and then shall I 'set My hand again the second time,' and gather them in that migrated with Jonah, the son of Amittai, to the land of Pathros, and those that dwell in the land of Shinar, Hamath, Elam, and the islands of the sea."

When Moses had heard this, he departed from heaven with a joyous spirit. The Angel of Death followed him to earth but could not possess himself of

Moses' soul, for he refused to give it up to him, delivering it to none but God Himself.

The first step in the development of the Messiah idea in Judaism was the anointing of priests and kings. The Hebrew word for Messiah (moshah) *means "anointed." The Greek term is* Christos. *Priests and kings were anointed with holy oil and were sanctified as "messiahs" or "anointed ones."*

The second phase of the development of the Messiah idea in Judaism was (and is, for Orthodox Jews) the belief in the coming of a personal Messiah. He would be preceded by the return to earth of Elijah the prophet. The Messiah, the anointed one, would be a descendant of the house of David. His advent would be preceded by "the pangs of the Messiah," a period of suffering, trial, and tribulation. The Messiah, according to tradition, would enter Jerusalem riding upon a white ass and would be proclaimed as "King of the Jews." Christianity accepts the revered belief that Joshua was the Messiah. In the Hebrew, "Joshua" means "savior." The Greek word for "Joshua" is "Jesus." Orthodox Judaism claims that the Messiah has not as yet appeared. According to this belief, when the Messiah does appear, there will be no more suffering, war, poverty, or death. Those who have died will be resurrected and will live forever.

Reform, or Liberal Judaism, does not accept this point of view. As a result of its theological conclusions, there is a third step to the development of the Messiah idea in Judaism, and that is a messianic age rather than a Messiah. Reform Judaism does not look for a supernatural coming of a personal Messiah. It looks forward to a messianic era of universal justice, brotherhood, and peace. Each individual must consecrate himself to make God's kingdom on earth a reality by obedience to the commandments of God, and by the application of religion to life.

Such a point of view is amply substantiated by the Jewish midrashic tradition.

❧ Rabbi Jochanan ben Zakkai taught: "If you hold a seedling in your hand and you hear the people shout, 'The Messiah has come,' you must plant the seedling first, and then go out to welcome the Messiah."

As opposed to the belief that the Messiah would come at a fixed time, there evolved another doctrine that the date was not fixed but would be affected by the conduct of the people.

❧ The rabbis read into the words of Isaiah, "I the Lord will hasten it in its time," which were explained in this sense: "If you are worthy I will hasten it; if you are not worthy, it will be in its time."

Man must, through his own efforts, help to bring about the messianic age.

❧ When a disciple of the rabbi of Lentshno visited the rabbi of Kotsk, his host said to him: "Give my greetings to your teacher. I love him very much. But why does he cry to God to send the Messiah? Why does he not rather cry to Israel to turn to God? It is written: 'Wherefore criest thou unto Me? speak unto the children of Israel.' "

❧ Rabbi Hiyya Rabbah inquired the real meaning of the verse "And God said: 'Let there be light.' " The sages answered: "This is God's challenge to man to assist in establishing the messianic era. That is what is meant by the verse from Isaiah, 'Arise, shine, for thy light is come, and the glory of the Lord is risen upon thee.' "

The hope for the messianic era is beautifully expressed in the Reform prayer book:

May the time not be distant, O God, when Thy name shall be worshiped in all the earth, when unbelief shall disappear and error be no more. Fervently we pray that the day may come when all men shall invoke Thy name, when corruption and evil shall give way to purity and goodness, when superstition shall no longer enslave the mind, nor idolatry blind the eye, when all who dwell on earth shall know that to Thee alone every knee must bend and every tongue give homage. O may all, created in Thine image, recognize that they are brethren, so that one in spirit and one in fellowship, they may be forever united before Thee. Then shall Thy kingdom be established on earth and the word of Thine ancient seer be fulfilled: The Lord will reign forever and ever. On that day the Lord shall be One and His name shall be One.

The third phase of the messianic concept in Judaism may be summed up as follows:

There was a rabbi who met Elijah, the wandering spirit of prophecy. He asked: "When will the Messiah come?" Elijah answered: "Today, if ye will but so live."

The very word "Christianity" means "the religion of the Messiah"—a religion that looks to the future for the fulfillment of the messianic age. Judaism is predicated on the hope for the future fulfillment of the messianic age. Although there are differences in theology, both religions join in the ethical effort to build God's kingdom on earth. By this effort both religions attest to their hope for man's future.

Chapter IX

HOPE

"And there is hope for thy future, saith the Lord"
(Jeremiah 31:17).

Today there are many voices of doom and prophets of
defeatism predicting the end of our civilization. They offer a
future of atomic destruction and cosmic death, even as they
implore:

> Let not the atom bomb
> Be the final sequel
> In which all men
> Are cremated equal.

Many are the poets, novelists, theologians, and philosophers who have become literary pied pipers, leading the

211

children of God in a rat race to oblivion. They bespeak the
voice of doom. Echoing through the ages there is another
voice—the still small voice of divinity, summoning man to
hope, to create, to build a future that will reveal God's
kingdom of justice, brotherhood, and peace for all the peoples
and nations of the world. Which voice will we heed?

There is a force in the world that is mightier than the atom.
It can have a greater impact than the bomb. That force is the
power of a living, dynamic, religious faith—a faith that can
transform society into God's kingdom on earth.

This sacred ideal, which has been enunciated by religious
prophets and dreamers through the ages, may be attained.
Man has the religious matériel with which he may fashion the
good society envisaged by Isaiah and Jesus. There is sufficient
man power, woman power, and God power available to unite
the peoples and nations of the world into one great brotherhood. Such a concept of world brotherhood, however, requires
a religious understanding of the right to be different, and a
clear distinction between uniformity and unity.

THE RIGHT TO BE DIFFERENT

Hope for the future of man demands an emphasis upon
unity rather than uniformity, and a recognition of the validity
of differences, whether they are religious, national, or racial.
It is the harmonization of these differences that will create a
symphony of religious brotherhood. The insistence upon
conformity will result in a cacophony of conflict.

Rabbinic literature teaches that coins that are minted from
the same pattern are alike, while men and women—descendants of Adam and Eve—are different. It is further insisted
that, to achieve brotherhood, differences must be respected and
accepted with love.

ೀ In a commentary to the book of Numbers (27:14), the rabbis taught that when Moses was about to ascend the mountaintop, knowing that he was to be replaced as leader of Israel, "Moses spoke unto the LORD, saying: 'Let the LORD, the God of the spirits of all flesh, set a man over the congregation.' " The rabbis inquired into the meaning of this, declaring, "The God of the spirits of all flesh, is a God who knows the varying spirits of men and who therefore knows what type of spirit is required in the man who is to fill the place of Moses." According to the rabbis, Moses prayed: "Sovereign of the universe, Thou knowest the minds of all men and how the mind of one man differs from that of another. Appoint over them a leader who will be able to bear with the differing minds of every one of Thy children."

Here, the right to differ is not only recognized but required as a qualification for religious leadership. Man is not to be placed upon a Procrustean bed of conformity, with the purpose of ironing out differences. A requisite for the leadership of the children of Israel is the ability to bear with a diversity of opinion and conviction.

The rabbis were intrigued with the biblical account of the destruction of the wicked cities of Sodom and Gomorrah. What was the nature of their sin? Why did these cities merit destruction even though Abraham had interceded in their behalf with such eloquence and persuasion?

The sin of Sodom was the insistence upon conformity. The inhabitants of both Sodom and Gomorrah manifested a xenophobia that compelled them to forbid kindness to any stranger. Without compassion, they harassed and tortured all those who came into their midst.

ೀ The cruelty of the Sodomites was without measure. Lot had a daughter, Paltit, so named because she had been born to him shortly after he escaped captivity through the help of Abraham. Paltit lived in Sodom, where she had married. Once a beggar came to town, and the court issued a proclamation that none should give him anything to eat, in order that he might die of starvation. But Paltit had pity upon the unfortunate wretch, and every day when she went to the well to draw water, she supplied him with a piece of bread, which she hid in her water pitcher. The inhabitants of the two sinful cities, Sodom and Gomorrah, could not understand why the beggar did not perish, and they suspected that someone was giving him food in secret. Three men concealed themselves near the beggar and caught Paltit in the act of giving him something to eat. She had to pay for her humanity with death; she was burned upon a pyre.

When strangers entered Sodom and Gomorrah they were given gold, silver, and precious jewels. However, requests for food were met with stubborn refusal. The stranger might offer precious jewels for a crust of bread, but such entreaties were met with jeers and blows. Ultimately, strangers died of starvation, after which the gold and jewels were confiscated by the officials, to be used again in enticing other hapless visitors.

When a stranger appeared in Sodom and Gomorrah, the officials put him in a bed they had placed in the town square. If he was too short for the bed, they would stretch and pull his legs and body until he was the length of the bed. If he was too long for the bed, they cut off his legs to make him fit into it.

The sin of Sodom and Gomorrah, according to the rabbis, was the sin of conformity. They insisted that everyone think

as they did and act as they did. *There could be no differences
in Sodom and Gomorrah — no differences of worship, or belief,
or action. That is why these cities were doomed to destruction,
despite the pleas of Abraham, who interceded for his enemies.*

THE DEMOCRATIC WAY OF LIFE

*According to the rabbis, Moses learned an important lesson
in democracy from a stranger and an alien to Israel. The man
who taught him was his father-in-law, Jethro, the Kenite
priest.*

⚘ "And when Moses' father-in-law saw all that he did
to the people [judging them day and night], he said:
'What is this thing that thou doest to the people? Why
sittest thou thyself alone, and all the people stand about
thee from morning unto even?' " When Moses protested, Jethro admonished him, saying, "for the thing is
too heavy for thee; thou art not able to perform it
thyself alone." He advised Moses to select out rulers
and judges to judge the people at all seasons.

*From this the rabbis derived the tradition that no man must
take it upon himself to be sole judge. There must be provided
many judges to allow for many shades of opinion and a
diversity of conviction. It was made clear to Israel that the
Torah and the knowledge of God may not be limited to one
class or to one group. The following homily illustrates the
belief that the revelation of God belongs to all.*

⚘ Rabbi Jannai once rebuked an ignorant man for his
lack of religious learning. The man said: "You have
mine inheritance, which you are withholding from
me!" "What inheritance?" cried the rabbi. "Once when

I passed a school," answered the man, "I heard the voices of children reciting: 'The Torah which Moses commanded us is the inheritance of the congregation of Jacob' (Deuteronomy 33:4). It is not written 'the congregation of Rabbi Jannai,' but 'the congregation of Jacob.' "

Other rabbis elaborated upon this story to teach that the Torah is not the inheritance of one rabbi alone, or of the congregation of Jacob alone, but belongs to all the children of God.

"Every man must be judged on the scale of merit" is a favorite statement in rabbinic Judaism. Justice must be meted out equitably without regard to a man's wealth, influence, or social position. No individual who evaluates another may accept hearsay or biased opinion. He must make his own observation and judge without prejudice.

🦁 "The Lord came down to see [the town of Babel]" (Genesis 11:5). But did He need to come down? Is not all revealed to Him who knows what is in the darkness and with whom light dwells? The answer is that God did this as a lesson to mankind, not to pass sentence, yea, not even to utter a word, on hearsay, but to look with their own eyes.

In a democracy the weak must be protected. In a family of nations the smallest and weakest nation has equal rights with the largest and most powerful. Commenting on the biblical verse "In righteousness shalt thou judge thy neighbor," the Dubner Maggid told the following parable:

🦁 Once upon a time a plague was raging among the animals. The lion, considered the king of beasts, decided to hold a trial and find out who among all the

animals was responsible for this dreadful plague, because it must be due to some sin that had been
committed. Thereupon the animals were summoned to
his presence, and when asked about their respective
sins, they confessed. It was now the turn of the bear,
the wolf, and the tiger. They confessed that they tore
asunder, mutilated, and killed animals and humans
without mercy. The verdict was "not guilty," and they
were exonerated from all blame by the lion, who simply
said that what they did was only their duty and
function.

At last it was the turn of the lamb to appear before the
court. She began to wonder what wrong she had done,
when suddenly she remembered that on one occasion,
because she was very hungry, she saw some straw
sticking out of the shepherd's shoe and ate it. That was
it, then. The lamb, without any further investigation,
was at once condemned, judged, and pronounced
guilty. "For her sin," roared the lion, "has this terrible
disaster befallen us all."

*The Dubner Maggid used this parable to excoriate those
who exonerate themselves of their own sins, even as they hold
guilty the weak for minor offenses committed.*

THE BROTHERHOOD OF MAN

*The expression "the fatherhood of God and the brotherhood
of man" is one of the most frequently used in our churches and
synagogues when we wish to show the unity of man under
God. While the phrase is facile on our lips, to what extent do
we put it in practice? Do we really believe it? Do we really
observe it?*

The watchword of the Jewish faith not only declares the

unity of God, but its corollary conclusion. If God is the Creator, our Heavenly Father, then all men are His children and are thus bound together in the uncommon bond of brotherhood. Here is the great challenge to Judaism and Christianity, to all religious faiths that proclaim the fatherhood of God and the brotherhood of man. If this is but a phrase, then we make a mockery of religion. If this is basic doctrine, then everyone who calls himself a Christian or a Jew is committed to apply his religious faith to the end that all men shall be united in brotherhood. To achieve this, man must attain spiritual maturity, and the will to live by and beyond his faith. Man must behold his fellow man in the universal perspective of divinity.

In rabbinic Judaism the term "neighbor" was intended to include all human beings. It was accepted Jewish belief that "the Jewish community must provide for the poor of the Gentiles along with the Jewish poor; such Gentiles are to be visited as are the Jewish sick, and burial shall be accorded the Gentile dead as well as the Jewish dead." Rabbi Jochanan ben Zakkai was always the first to greet everyone he met, even the heathen whom he encountered for the first time in the marketplace.

🏵 The rabbi of Sassov once gave the last money he had in his pocket to a man of ill repute. His disciples threw it up to him. He answered them: "Shall I be more finicky than God, who gave it to me?"

Rabbinic tradition admonishes: "Say not, 'I will love scholars, but hate their disciples,' or even 'I will love the disciples and hate the ignorant,' but love all, for he who hates his neighbor is as bad as a murderer. During the days of the second Temple, even though men studied Torah and gave to charity, they hated each other—and for this reason was the holy Temple destroyed." This is similarly expressed in the statement in I John 4:20: "If a man say, I love God, and hateth his brother, he is a liar."

According to the Talmud the real meaning given by the rabbis to the command "Love thy neighbor as thyself" is this:

🦬 "Put thyself in his place and act properly. As thou dost not desire to be robbed of thy property or thy good name, or to be injured, so do not these things to thy neighbor." The closing words, "I am the LORD thy God," were interpreted to mean an oath of God: "I am the LORD who created thy neighbor as well as thee. Therefore, if thou showest love to him, I shall surely reward thee with love."

The Talmud also states: "If two men claim thy help, and one is thy enemy, help him first." In the ancient Jewish prayer book this was to be recited before the morning prayer: "Lo, I solemnly promise to obey the command 'Thou shalt love thy neighbor as thyself'—O God, forgive, I pray Thee, those who have wronged me; forgive them in this world, and in the next." Before bowing himself before God in reverence, the Jew was then enjoined to purify his heart of all hatred or thoughts of vengeance toward his enemies.

🦬 In the second century, Rabbi Akiba, son of Joseph, was asked about the greatest principle of Judaism. He said it was the commandment in Leviticus, "Thou shalt love thy neighbor as thyself."

When God said, "neighbor," He did not specify the neighbor's religion, nationality, or the color of his skin.

🦬 His friend Rabbi Simeon, son of Azzai, disagreed. He said that the greatest verse is from Genesis: "This is the book of the generations of man. In the day that God created man, in the likeness of God made He him."

"This is the book of the generations of man." God's word is meant for all people, not for one religion alone, one race alone, or one nation. All men share the sacred image of God.

Micah said: "It hath been told thee, O man, . . . what the Lord doth require of thee: only to do justly, and to love mercy, and to walk humbly with thy God." The Jewish teachers point out that the Jews are not specified. This is consistent with the universalism of the Jewish faith. "It hath been told thee, O man"—not O Jew, O Christian, O Moslem—not O white race, O black race, O yellow race—not O America, O England, O Israel, O Judea—but O man.

We recall this same universalism in the Ten Commandments: "Thou shalt not kill." "Thou shalt not steal." "Thou shalt honor thy father and thy mother." The moral commands of God are obligations for all peoples, races, and religions.

The Talmud teaches that every phrase which issued from the mouth of the All-powerful divided itself into seventy languages. Hence, Moses expounded the Torah in seventy languages.

The exposition of Talmudic universalism is revealed in the comments on the verse "Ye shall therefore keep My statutes, and Mine ordinances, which if a man do, he shall live by them" (Leviticus 18:5). Whence is it deduced that even a Gentile who obeys the Torah is the equal of the high priest? From the words "which if a man do he shall live by them." Similarly it is said, "This is the law of mankind, Lord God" (II Samuel 7:19). It is not stated, "This is the law of the priests, or the Levites, or of Israel," but "the law of mankind." In like manner it is not stated, "Open the gates, that priests or Levites or Israel may enter," but "Open the gates that a righteous Gentile keeping faithfulness may enter" (Isaiah

26:2). *Furthermore, it is not stated, "This is the gate of the* LORD; *priests or Levites or Israel shall enter into it," but "The righteous shall enter into it" (Psalm 118:20). In the same way it is not stated, "Rejoice in the* LORD, *O ye priests or Levites or Israel," but "Rejoice in the* LORD, *O ye righteous" (Psalm 33:1), and it is not stated, "Do good, O* LORD, *to the priests or Levites or Israel" but "unto the good" (Psalm 125:4).*

We note, too, that the usual benediction uttered is introduced with "Blessed art Thou, O Lord our God, King of the universe" —not King of Israel, or King of the Jews alone.

The sacrifices in the Temple were intended for the whole of humanity. "On the eighth day of the Feast of Tabernacles, seventy bullocks were offered on behalf of the seventy nations."

The doors of the Temple of God must never be bolted against anyone who desires admittance from pure motives. That is why Isaiah declared: "My house shall be called a house of prayer for all peoples." That is why Malachi declared: "Have we not all one father? Hath not one God created us? Why do we deal treacherously every man against his brother?"

A merchant once came to Rabbi Meir Shalom, a son of Rabbi Yehoshua Asher, and complained of another merchant who had opened his shop right next door to him. "You seem to think," said the zaddik, "that it is your shop that supports you, and you are setting your heart upon it instead of on God, who is your support. But perhaps you do not know where God lives? It is written: 'Love thy neighbor as thyself: I am the LORD.' This means: 'You shall want for your neighbor what he needs, just as you do for yourself—and therein you will find the Lord.' "

A scholarly man said to Rabbi Abraham of Stretyn: "It is said that you give people strange drugs and that your drugs are most marvelous. Give me one such drug that I may attain to the fear of the Lord."

"I know of no such drug," said Rabbi Abraham. "But if you wish I can give you one for the love of God."

"All the better!" exclaimed the other. "Just you see that I get it."

"It is the love of one's fellow man," answered the rabbi.

Sometimes we mistakenly believe that we have to do something dramatic to demonstrate our zeal for brotherhood. Frequently all that is required is a kind word or a loving heart.

A beautiful story from Jewish lore illustrates the nobility and holiness of brotherhood.

🦁 Ephraim, an aged farmer of Palestine, called his sons, Joseph and Samuel, to appear before him. He said: "My sons, I am about to die and I bequeath all my possessions to you to be divided equally. You, Joseph, shall inherit the tract on the east, and you, Samuel, shall inherit the tract on the west. I adjure you to live in brotherly love." The father died and the sons separated, each to till the soil bequeathed unto him. Joseph, the elder, had a wife and seven sons; Samuel never married and was childless.

It happened many years later that Joseph thought of his brother living on his farm. He said to himself: "My brother is lonely and has no sons to assist him. Perhaps he will not have enough food for the winter. I know what I will do. I will take sheaves and carry them to my brother without his knowledge, and perhaps that will help him during the difficult winter months."

It so happened that at the same time Samuel was thinking about his brother and he said to himself: "My brother Joseph has a wife and seven sons. Who knows whether they will have enough to eat when winter comes? I know what I will do. I will take six sheaves to my brother's field without his knowledge."

In the morning Joseph, as was his custom, counted his sheaves and found the number to be the same. He was surprised because he knew that he had removed six sheaves and taken them to his brother Samuel. Samuel, too, counted his sheaves and was surprised to find that he had the same number, even though he had taken six sheaves to his brother Joseph.

After considering the matter, Joseph said: "I will take twelve sheaves this time to my brother Samuel, without his knowledge." Samuel said the same thing: "This time I will take twelve sheaves to my brother Joseph." The next day both brothers were perplexed as they counted the sheaves and discovered that the same number remained.

Joseph determined now that he would use a donkey, and he placed a large bundle of sheaves upon the beast of burden, planning to transport the sheaves during the night. Samuel planned the same thing, and he placed a large bundle of sheaves upon his donkey. When night fell each brother started for the farm of the other. Halfway they met. Upon discovering that each was attempting to help the other, they fell in each other's arms and wept.

On the very spot where the brothers met, and on the soil that received their tears, God determined that this should be the site of the Temple in Jerusalem, for in truth brotherly love sanctified the soil and consecrated the land as a hallowed place of God.

Both biblical and rabbinic Judaism teach that it is a sin against God "to stand idly by the blood of thy neighbor" (Leviticus 19:16).

*In response to Cain's inquiry "Am I my brother's keeper?"
God answered: "The voice of thy brother's blood crieth unto
Me from the ground" (Genesis 4:10).*

🔯 Rabbi Simeon ben Yohai taught: "This may be compared to the case of men on a ship, one of whom took
a borer and began boring beneath his own place. His
fellow travelers said to him: 'What are you doing?' Said
he to them: 'What does that matter to you? Am I not
boring under my own place?' Said they: 'Because the
water will come up and flood the ship for us all.' What
we do influences the security of our fellow men. Man is
ever responsible for his brother's welfare."

*Man is responsible for his brother. God holds man account-
able for sins committed against his fellow man.*

🔯 From the depths of the pit Joseph appealed to his
brethren, saying: "O my brethren, what have I done
unto you, and what is my transgression? Why are you
not afraid before God on account of your treatment of
me? Am I not flesh of your flesh, and bone of your
bone? Jacob your father, is he not also my father? Why
do you act thus toward me? And how will you be able
to lift up your countenance before Jacob? O Judah,
Reuben, Simon, Levi, my brethren, deliver me, I pray
you, from the dark place into which you have cast me.
Though I committed a trespass against you, yet are ye
children of Abraham, Isaac, and Jacob, who were
compassionate with the orphan, gave food to the hungry, and clothed the naked. How, then, can ye withhold your pity from your own brother, your own flesh
and bone? And though I sinned against you, yet you
will hearken unto my petition for the sake of my father.

O that my father knew what my brethren are doing unto me, and what they spake unto me!"

To avoid hearing Joseph's weeping and cries of distress, his brethren passed on from the pit and stood at a bowshot's distance.

How often do we anesthetize our sensitivities to avoid the pain of others! How frequently do we stand at a distance and avert our eyes from the hands and hearts that reach out to us for help!

Ignorance is never accepted as an excuse for ignoring the needs of our brethren. Indifference is never acceptable to God. To be prejudiced against one's fellow man is to discriminate against the Divine image. The rabbis of the Talmud would have concurred with Bishop Vincent S. Waters, of North Carolina, who said, "Souls don't have color." According to the Midrash, souls are not to be thought of in terms of race, nationality, sex, or sectarian designation.

The following story from the Jewish tradition is also to be found in Indian folklore.

A patriarch who was about to die did not know which of his four sons should receive his inheritance and be elevated to the leadership of the community. He said, "Go forth, my sons, pioneer into the unknown, and bring me back some tangible sign of how far you have progressed."

The first son started out and came to a seemingly impenetrable forest. He could not go on, and so he picked a bramble bush and returned with it to his father. The second son came to the forest and went through it until he came to a turbulent stream. He picked some moss from the bank and returned with it to his father. The third son traversed the forest and by persistent effort crossed the turbulent stream, but was stopped by a towering mountain. He picked a flower that grew at the base of the mountain and returned with it to his father.

The fourth son, even more persistent, went through the forest, crossed the turbulent stream, and confronted by the mountain, determined to make the steep ascent. He paused for a moment of prayer and then, revitalized, started up the mountainside, slowly and tortuously. He fell, but scrambled to his feet and persisted upward until, bruised and bleeding, he stood on the mountaintop. He looked up and he looked down, and then he returned to his father.

This son said to his father, "I have climbed to the very top of the mountain, and O my father, I looked up and felt so close to God that I wanted to reach up and to touch Him. And then I looked down and saw little specks below, and I realized that they were more than specks—they were men and women. And even more than men and women, they were my brothers and my sisters. I have brought you back nothing tangible except an exalted vision of the fatherhood of God and the brotherhood of all men."

Perhaps we, in our journey through life, may not bring to our Heavenly Father tangible material possessions, but if we bring to Him a glorious vision of the fatherhood of God and the brotherhood of all men, we will have climbed, through prayer and through consecrated religious effort, to the place where God may be seen—to the highest mountaintop of divinity.

The Hasidic movement extended its vision beyond the Jewish people and the Jewish faith, to behold man in the perspective of universalism. Even though zealous for the peoplehood of all Israel, the teachings of the Hasidic rabbis

*were not limited to Jews and Judaism, but were meant to apply
to all peoples and all faiths.*

*Because he is privileged to be identified with the covenant
God made at Sinai, the Jew must ever remember that he is
bound to God in love. It is because of that covenant, and it is
because of his love for God—the Creator, the Father of all—
that he must extend his love to every human being created in
the image of God.*

⚜ One day a rich but miserly man came seeking
counsel from a rabbi. Indicating a window which faced
the street, the rabbi asked, "What do you see from the
window?"

"People," answered the rich man.

The rabbi then led him to a mirror in the room. "And
what do you see now?" he asked.

"Now I see myself," answered the rich man.

Then the rabbi said: "Behold, in the window there is
a glass, and in the mirror there is a glass. But the glass
of the mirror is covered with a little silver, and no
sooner is the silver added than you cease to see others
but see only yourself."

*It was not the quest for gold that concerned the Hasidim. It
was the quest for God that animated their endeavors and filled
their hearts with a sense of Divine purpose. If a person is
interested in himself alone—his needs, his ambitions, his
material desires—how can he go beyond himself to devote
his life to service to others? How can he even see others if his
vision is limited to himself? Thus, each individual must
decide whether he will look upon life as a mirror, concerned
solely with himself and the reflection he sees—or whether he
will look through the window of a living faith and extend his
vision to behold humanity. It is this vision of humanity that*

*must challenge those of the Jewish faith to labor for a sacred
cause, to fulfill the destiny and mission of Israel as servants of
the holy God.*

*The Jew was summoned to behold people and life through
the perspective of eternity, and by so doing to sensitize his
vision to behold all men as the children of God.*

*The question is frequently asked: "Does Judaism send out
missionaries?" The answer is "No." Judaism is a religion with
a mission, but with no missionaries. Despite a period in
history when the Pharisees attempted to make converts from
paganism to a belief in a God of morality, Judaism has not
sought proselytes.*

*One reason for this is the pervading universalism of the
Jewish faith. Believing that God is the universal Father and
that all men are His children, Judaism has never thought in
terms of one, true religion. As long as men obey the will of
God, they should cleave to their own faith. There are many
different roads to the kingdom of heaven. Truth is universal.
God's love is universal and is bestowed upon all who seek Him
in truth.*

*Judaism will accept those who seek admission to the Jewish
faith in sincerity and in love.*

*The following midrash, while shocking, indicates the rab-
binic belief that to become a proselyte is to be spiritually
reborn.*

A woman once came to Rabbi Eliezer to be made a
proselyte, saying to him, "Rabbi, receive me." He said
to her, "Recount your acts to me in confession." She
told him: "My youngest son was conceived through my
eldest son." He stormed at her; so she went to Rabbi
Joshua, who received her. His disciples said to him:
"Rabbi Eliezer drove her away and you accept her!" He
replied, "When she set her mind on being a proselyte,

she no longer lived to the world." That is, the woman by her repentance died to her past life and would never live in it again.

It is further declared that the Holy One, blessed be He, greatly loves the proselytes. To what may this be compared? To a king who had a flock which used to go out to the field and come in at evening. So it was each day. Once a stag came in with the flock. He associated with the goats and grazed with them. When the flock came in to the fold, he came in with them; when they went out to graze, he went out with them. The king was told: "A certain stag has joined the flock and is grazing with them every day. He goes out with them and comes in with them." The king felt an affection for him. When he went out into the field, the king gave orders: "Let him have good pasture, such as he likes; no man shall beat him; be careful with him!" When he came in with the flock, the king also would tell them, "Give him to drink"; and he loved him very much.

The servants said to the king: "Sovereign! You possess so many he-goats, you possess so many lambs, you possess so many kids, and you never caution us about them; yet you give us instructions every day about this stag!"

Said the king to them: "The flock have no choice, whether they want or not, it is their nature to graze in the field all day and to come in at even to sleep in the fold. The stags, however, sleep in the wilderness. It is not in their nature to come into places inhabited by man. Shall we then not account it as a merit to this one which has left behind the whole of the broad, vast wilderness, the abode of all the beasts, and has come to stay in the courtyard?"

In like manner, ought we not to be grateful to the

proselyte who has left behind him his family and his father's house, aye, has left behind his people and all the other peoples of the world, and has chosen to come to us? Accordingly, God has provided him with special protection, for He exhorted Israel that they should be, and so indeed it says: "Love ye therefore the proselyte" (Deuteronomy 10:19); "And a proselyte shall thou not oppress" (Exodus 23:9; cf. Leviticus 19:33–34).

⁑ Maimonides, the Jewish philosopher, said: "You asked about the Gentiles. Keep in mind that 'God requires the heart,' and everything depends on the intention of the heart. Therefore . . . there is no doubt that he who achieves ethical qualities in the right ways of life and the right wisdom of belief in God, merits the future world, and so our teachers said: 'A heathen who studies the Torah is equal to the high priest.' "

While I was conducting services for the men in the armed forces at Fort Custer, Michigan, it happened that a young man of the Protestant faith was in emergency need of a chaplain. Since the Protestant chaplain was on leave, the Catholic chaplain went to see the boy. The soldier was somewhat apprehensive and said: "Father, I appreciate your coming to see me, but I am a Protestant. I hope you won't try to change my faith."

The Roman Catholic chaplain said with a gentle smile: "My son, I don't want you to change your faith. I want your faith to change you!"

That, too, is the Jewish hope: not to change any man's faith—but to look to God with the prayer that man's faith may change him, inspire him, and challenge him to enter into a Divine partnership.

MAN AS COPARTNER OF GOD

✄ The rabbis commented on the verse from Ezekiel, "I will remove the stony heart out of their flesh." This recalls the story of a huge boulder which blocked a road, preventing people from passing. When they complained to the king, he said: "You chip it away yourselves, bit by bit, and then I shall remove it altogether." Man must serve as a partner of God in shaping the future.

This means that each individual must contribute his best efforts to the building of God's kingdom.

✄ There was a king who invited his subjects to a banquet. He told each guest to bring a flask of wine and informed each that his wine would be poured into a large wine vat. Each one thought: "What will my small flask of wine mean? I will bring a flask of water and no one will know the difference." When the guests were assembled at the banquet, the king summoned his servants to serve the guests with the contents of the barrel. Each one was served water, for they all had said: "What will my small flask of wine mean? I will bring a flask of water and no one will know the difference."

✄ The rabbis taught that each one must bring his best efforts to the building of a good society. Let no man say: "What will my small share mean?" for if everyone thinks in that way, how can we serve the future?

✄ Once there was a good man who wanted to do good. One day he noticed the miserable conditions in which a certain poor carpenter lived. The rich man called the carpenter in and commissioned him to build a beautiful house. "I want this to be an ideal cottage. Use only the best materials, employ only the best workmen, and spare no expense." He said that he was going on a journey and that he hoped the house would be finished when he returned.

The carpenter saw this as his great opportunity. Therefore, he skimped on materials, he hired inferior workers at low wages and covered their mistakes with paint, and he cut corners wherever he could.

When the rich man returned, the carpenter brought him the key and said: "I have followed your instructions and built your house as you told me to." "I'm glad," said the rich man; and handing the key back to the builder, he continued, "Here are the keys. They are yours. I had you build this house for yourself. You and your family are to have it as my gift."

In the years that followed, the carpenter never ceased to regret the way in which he had cheated himself. "Had I known," he would say to himself, "that I was building this house for myself . . ."

There are some who, when called upon to help build the future, try to avoid the cost of concentrated effort and do not give their best. They fail to understand that they are building for themselves and their children.

Rabbi Ishmael and Rabbi Akiba were walking by the way when they met a sick man. Beholding a farmer plowing his field nearby, Rabbi Ishmael asked the farmer to summon a physician.

"O rabbi of little faith," said the farmer, "it is God's will that this man has become ill. If God wants him to die, he will die. If God wants him to live, he will live."

"What hast thou in thy hand?" inquired the rabbi. "A plow, of course," answered the farmer. The rabbi said:

"Why do you interfere with the earth which God has created? O farmer of little faith, if God wants your crops to grow, they will grow. If God does not want your crops to grow, they will not grow. But what do you do? You enter into copartnership with God in the work of creation. Thus it is with the physician, who is a co-partner with God in the work of healing. Go and summon a physician."

Not only physicians but those of every occupation must regard themselves as copartners with God.

APPLIED RELIGION

Two thousand years ago Rabbi Simeon ben Gamaliel taught: "Not the expounding of the Torah is the chief thing, but the doing of it."

Rabbi Hiyya said: "If a man occupies himself with the study of the Torah without the intention of fulfilling it, it were better he had never been born."

Another sage said: "He who occupies himself with the study of the Torah only is as if he had no God."

The exalted purpose of applied religion is to enable man to achieve this Divine partnership with God in the building of a God-directed society.

Anyone who retires from the world and its problems is like a man who says: "What have I to do with the concerns of the community or the world? What have I to do with their suits? Why must I listen to their talk? Peace to my soul"—such a man destroys the world.

Thus, for a man to resign from his Divine destiny of building God's kingdom is to repudiate God.

In a significantly cogent analysis of the verse "Ye are the children of the LORD your God" (Deuteronomy 14:1), the rabbis use the Hebrew text to convey a new meaning.

☕ The Hebrew word for children is *bonim*. The Hebrew word for builders is *boenim*. Because of the similarity of the words, the rabbis suggest that the passage may be translated "Ye are builders of the LORD." What is it that man must build? He must build God's kingdom on earth.

A further comment is made by Rabbi Judah. He said: "The people of Israel were only 'children of God' so long as they conformed to the Divine will, and they forfeited the honor when they were disobedient."

Rabbi Meir dissented, saying: "Just as a father loves his children even though they may disobey him, so whether their conduct is filial or unfilial, men can never cease being children of the Lord. God waits in love for His children to fulfill their function of being His builders."

Jewish custom requires that the readings of the prophets in the synagogue must not end on a note of gloom and despair. Accordingly, we note that only verse 4 of chapter 3 of Jeremiah is read in the synagogue, "Didst thou not just now cry unto me: 'My father, Thou art the friend of my youth'?" In chapter 4 only verses 1 and 2 are included, to show the hope for Israel's return to God and the spiritual regeneration of all humanity.

A child of God must never give up hope for the future. Such pessimism is a negation of God. It suggests that God's purposes are not fulfilled.

The history of Israel might be written with a pen dipped into tears. Despite thousands of years of persecution and suffering, the Jew is admonished to hear the clarion call of

Zechariah, "Return to the stronghold, ye prisoners of hope."
No matter how dark the hour, the Jew was commanded to
hope in God and to remember that his golden age was not in
the past—but shall yet be in a future under the sovereignty of
God.

✥ When Abraham was childless, he cried out to God in
his distress, beseeching the Lord to grant him offspring.
God said: "Thy seed shall be as numerous as the sand
upon the shore." Abraham remained disconsolate and
said: "Almighty God, what care I if my descendants are
numerous and populate the east and the west, the
north and the south, as long as they do not perpetuate
the ideals Thou hast ordained." God answered: "Look
up, Abraham." Abraham looked up and beheld the
stars suffusing the inky oriental heavens with light.
"Thus shall be thy seed, Abraham; not only as numerous as the sand upon the shore, but like the stars of
the heaven bringing light—the light of learning, the
light of justice, the light of brotherhood—into the future." Then was Abraham content.

It is this hope that has sustained the Jew through all the
vicissitudes of history. Some have called this the messianic
hope. Some have called it a vision of God's kingdom on earth.
Is it possible for Jews to achieve this hope alone? Is this effort
to build God's kingdom limited to those of the Jewish faith? Or
do all the righteous have a share in the messianic world to
come?

JUDAISM AND CHRISTIANITY— RIVALS OR PARTNERS?

This volume began with the thesis that there is a reverently
uncommon denominator that unites Judaism and Christianity
in the quest for God. It concludes with the prayerful hope
that, as we hunger for the Divine, we may derive spiritual

sustenance from the Judaeo-Christian ethical tradition, and nurture our souls with understanding and love. True brotherhood means a commitment to one's own faith with loyalty and religious devotion. It next requires, not agreement with, but respect for the commitment of others to their faith. Interfaith must never mean the surrender of conviction, but the strengthening of conviction. It must lead us from darkness to light, from prejudice to understanding, from divisiveness to unity, from indifference to love.

Both Judaism and Christianity proclaim the fatherhood of God and the universality of Divine love. Believing this, what difference does it make to God the names by which He is called? What difference does it make to God the mode of ritual or the liturgical procedure, as long as His children seek Him in truth, join hands and hearts as brothers to obey His commandments, and fulfill the Divine destiny He has determined for man?

To comprehend this Divine destiny, we must constantly strive to sensitize our souls to the voice of God summoning us, challenging us to enter into a religious partnership to build the future. To some, the efforts of religious men and women to unite for a sacred purpose may appear futile and senseless. It may be compared to the story told by Rabbi Moshe Hayyim Ephraim:

🦌 "I heard this from my grandfather, the Baal Shem. Once a fiddler played so sweetly that all who heard him began to dance. A deaf man chanced along and looked through the window, and since he could not hear the music, the actions seemed to him the actions of madmen—senseless and futile."

Even though the religious efforts of men and women of good will appear to be futile and senseless to some, they must continue to advance the cause of human brotherhood despite the opposition of those who refuse to attune their souls to the music of divinity.

🔯 In a commentary on Genesis 28:12—"And he dreamed, and behold a ladder set up on the earth, and the top of it reached to heaven; and behold the angels of God ascending and descending on it"—the rabbis taught that Jacob attempted to climb the ladder unto heaven. As he was about to reach the top, ugly hands reached out to throw him to the earth. Again Jacob ascended to the top rungs, and again opposing hands reached out to prevent him from his heavenly ascent. A heavenly voice declared: "Jacob, you may not succeed in lifting yourself on high to God, but you and your descendants are charged with the sacred task of continuing your efforts to scale the ladder to Divinity."

So, even in our own generation, ugly hands of hate reach out to hinder man in his upward reach for God. Nonetheless, despite formidable opposition, man is charged with the sacred task of continuing the effort to climb heavenward to the Most High.

Brotherhood is no longer a moral luxury. It is a requisite for the survival of our civilization. That is why we must heed the warning of a story. It is not a Jewish story or a Christian story. It is the story of human beings in search of salvation:

🔯 In northern Minnesota, a farmer's five-year-old child was playing in the kitchen while his mother was busily engaged in her domestic chores. Unnoticed, the child toddled out of the house and out into the wheatfield.

Shortly thereafter, the mother noticed the absence of the child and began a frantic search for her baby. When she could not find the child in the immediate vicinity of the farmhouse, she called her husband and together they searched through the heaped-up sheaves of wheat. In desperation they summoned the farmhands and continued their search.

Several hours later, when the child still had not been found, the townspeople were called in and urged on by the entreaties of the father and mother. Those of every social position, economic level, and religious faith—the minister and the rabbi, the laborer and the millowner—beat at the sheaves of wheat, walking and running in every direction, with the hope of finding the child.

When this proved futile, someone suggested: "We seem to be going off in all directions. Why don't we join hands, form one large circle, spread out and then close in, encompassing every inch of the land?"

As the result, the preacher joined hands with the laboring man, and the physician joined hands with the town idler. Men of every station of life and of every faith joined hands to form a gigantic circle. Carefully examining every inch of the land, they narrowed the circle until someone reached down, picked up the child, and handed him to his father. After the physician had carefully examined the child, the father knew, by the look on his face, that the child was dead. He lifted the lifeless body of his child in his arms and cried out: "God, God—why didn't we join hands before it was too late?"

Because of the tensions that beset us, because of the threat of atomic destruction—we may no longer afford the luxury of going our separate ways. We must not incur the guilt that will rest upon each of us if, after the destruction of human lives, our Father in heaven should look upon the lifeless bodies of His children and ask us: "Why, despite your differences, did you not join together before it was too late?"

Therefore, if God's Divine purpose is to be fulfilled, it is imperative that Jews and Christians join hands, not as rivals, but as partners in the greatest spiritual building enterprise ever envisaged by man and ordained by the Lord: the building of God's kingdom on earth.

That is why the question "What seekest thou?" must be answered by each child of God, saying: "I seek my brethren!"

NAME INDEX

SUBJECT INDEX

ABOUT THE AUTHOR

Rabbi William B. Silverman, a master and doctor of Hebrew letters from Hebrew Union College, Cincinnati, has held pulpits in Nashville, Tennessee (where he was a leader in the civil rights movement); Kansas City, Missouri; and Palm Desert, California. A prolific writer, Rabbi Silverman has authored *The Still Small Voice: The Story of Jewish Ethics, The Still Small Voice Today: Jewish Ethical Living, God Help Me: From Kindergarten Religion to the Radical Faith,* and *When Mourning Comes: A Book of Comfort for the Grieving.*